SIGN
OF THE
FISH

NOEL DAVIDSON

AMBASSADOR

BELFAST, NORTHERN IRELAND
GREENVILLE, SOUTH CAROLINA

Sign of the Fish
© Copyright 2003 Noel Davidson

ISBN 1 84030 145 7

Ambassador Publications
a division of
Ambassador Productions Ltd.
Providence House
Ardenlee Street,
Belfast,
BT6 8QJ
Northern Ireland
www.ambassador-productions.com

Emerald House
427 Wade Hampton Blvd.
Greenville
SC 29609, USA
www.emeraldhouse.com

CONTENTS

INTRODUCTION

THE COLOURFUL BOOKLET which I had just been invited to read bore the title 'A Fisherman's Tale', but it was the subtitle that caught my eye. 'The story of what can happen when a business is wholly handed over to God,' it said. Well, what *can* happen when a business is wholly handed over to God? I wondered.

The question had me hooked.

On reading the story of the fish and chip shop described in the booklet I realised that there must be much more to it than I had yet discovered.

Would it make a book?

An introductory telephone call to August Ericson, the man whose father had been a fisherman, and whose own vision of becoming a fisher of men meant learning how to fry fish, soon convinced me that it would.

A dramatic evacuation during World War 2, a public school education, a crippling accident, a tender love story…. It seemed to possess all the vital ingredients. That, too, was only the start. The unusual conversion and even more unusual decision to sell up and go all out in business for God were yet to come. And the tales of what happened then, when August and his wife Jill bought over a shabby café in Sincil Street, Lincoln, were almost unbelievable. What would, or could happen, in a fish and chip shop adorned by texts? A restaurant with Bible verses on the menu and tracts on the tables?

August retired from business four years ago having produced thousands of fish suppers and mountains of mushy peas over nineteen years in Sign Of The Fish. He is now engaged in two leisure activities, both of which he enjoys, for they are both related to his deep love for his Lord. One is an interest in, and in depth study of, the nation of Israel in God's plan for the ages, and the other is the systematic distribution of Gospel literature in his native Grimsby.

The former fish fryer and I have met a number of times over the past few months and it has been a privilege to work with someone whose only aim is to live at the centre of God's will.

When discussing the name he and Jill had decided to call their business I asked August what was so special about the sign of the fish. His reply was a story in itself. It was one that I thought I knew, but was soon to find out that I didn't. At least not in full.

"Back in the days of the New Testament church, Christians faced persecution, and even execution, if they confessed their faith," August began, his passion for church history shining in his face. "So in order to discover if the strangers they often met were friends whom they could trust, the early believers used a secret sign. A Christian would engage the person he wasn't quite sure about in conversation. As they talked the Christian would be drawing away nonchalantly. The end result of his artistic doodling would be the outline of a fish, traced in the dust of the road with a staff or the toe of a sandal.

Then came the crucial bit," and August leaned forward to share it with me. It would be a pity if I missed it. "If the stranger was also a Christian he would complete the picture. He would step across and put the eye in, but if he…"

"Stop there, August. That's it!" I interrupted him.

"That's what?" my friend wanted to know, puzzled.

"That's what we have just been doing here for the last few months," I told him. "The writing of this book has been a partnership. You have been giving me the outline. Drawing the fish if you like. My job has just been to put the eye in to complete the picture. The final outcome will demonstrate that two men who had never met before can work together because they love one another in the Lord."

We both pray that you may find Sign Of The Fish a blessing and a challenge.

It has been to us.

Noel Davidson
June 2003.

SIDELINED AT SIXTEEN

1

It was heart-rending, that scream.

A number of the busy people bustling past stopped momentarily to see what had happened before hurrying on. It was a family thing, and nothing to do with them. They all had weighty matters on their minds. It was a case of survival. And the people of England were making their own arrangements.

The scene was the forecourt of Grimsby railway station. The month was September, and the year 1939.

War with Germany had just been declared.

The Ebenezersson family had come from Iceland to settle in the East coast fishing port some years before, and father had become a successful trawler captain. With the frightening prospect of war, and its expected toll of death and destruction looming up over the darkening horizon, Gwen, mother of the family, had become anxious for the safety of her five children. Grimsby would be on Hitler's hit list. She was firmly convinced of it.

The only sensible course of action, she reckoned was to send the three youngest boys back to Iceland for the duration of the conflict, however long, or short, that would be.

Although the parents had made some effort to explain the situation to their children, little August, the youngest of the three, couldn't understand it. His two older brothers, Valdi and Rabbee, seemed to accept it all with the chin-up chest-out stoicism required of 'brave big boys'. They were twelve and thirteen, after all.

To August though, at four years of age, it didn't make any sense.

Why would his mother want to send him away?

The emotional trauma of this parting at Grimsby railway station had now been magnified a million times by almost unbearable physical pain. His nineteen year old sister Kristen, the second oldest of the family and one of the two deemed mature enough to remain in England, had just closed the taxi door on his tiny hand.

Kristen was devastated. She began to kiss and hug her 'baby', as she called him. Her tears mingled with those of her dumbfounded 'little darling', as she pressed her cheek close to his.

Why were they doing this to him?

As the taxi pulled away from its rank August felt totally let down. He was being sent off into some vast unknown experience, and the only people who had ever loved him in his life were being left behind.

When the three evacuees arrived in Iceland on the boat from Hull, they were separated. Valdi and Rabbee were sent to a village on the west coast of the island to live with their grandparents, but August remained in Reykjavik, the capital, with his Aunt Sally.

Thus began a further trauma for the four-year old. Having been parted from his brothers was heartache enough but since they had been his last contact with the English language he was plunged into an even deeper dilemma. He couldn't communicate with anyone around him.

Aunt Sally did all she could to make the transition, which could never have been enjoyable, at least tolerable for the anguished August. But she couldn't speak English. And he didn't understand a word of Icelandic. Life in the rambling wooden house, which he was expected to call home, began as a nightmare.

He cried himself to sleep every night.

His aunt was a kind woman, however, and by consistent loving care gained the confidence of her little nephew. Gradually, too, he started to learn the language and respond to his aunt's compassionate attention.

In less than a year he began to feel like an Icelandic boy. England, which had become affected by the privations of war, was far away. It was little more than a distant, hazy memory. August began to look upon Aunt Sally as his mother.

When almost seven years of age he took his first job. Since his aunt was finding it difficult enough to feed and clothe the growing boy August realised that if he ever wanted to have any pocket money of his own he would have to make it. So he and his friend Todi began to sell newspapers on the streets of Reykjavik.

It was both hard work, and good fun for the two young entrepreneurs.

They called each evening at the newspaper office and collected twenty-six newspapers each to sell. The deal was that if they sold twenty-four papers they could keep, by way of commission, the price of the remaining two.

As he usually managed to sell his allocation most days August made enough money to keep him in sweets and treats. His business life had begun!

By October 1943 Hitler still hadn't made it to Grimsby, having obviously other more important places to bomb, and so August's parents decided that it was safe for him to return home. The problem was that by then August didn't want to go. Nor did his Aunt Sally want to let him go. He had become like a son to her, and she was acting 'mummy' to him.

It had to happen, though. There was a very tearful parting in Reykjavik and August, who was over eight, boarded the trawler 'Skallagrimur' for the return trip to Hull.

The voyage, which should normally have lasted four days at the most, took seven. There were two reasons for this. The first was that they had to keep constantly zigzagging to avoid the threat from the German U-boats. The other was the cold, clinging fog that wet everyone through and through and made navigation difficult. August was one of the few who didn't mind the fog for because of it the skipper gave him an 'important' task to perform. It was his duty to keep the ship's bell ringing almost constantly. After three days the fog lifted and the young mariner was excited to discover that they were surrounded by huge American Liberty ships. Then on the next day an anxious chill went around the trawler when a submarine broke the surface just ahead of them. The fear was replaced by a huge sigh of relief when it was discovered that it was part of a British patrol.

When the 'Skallagrimur' eventually docked in Hull, August's parents were waiting on the quayside. The returning exile recognised his father immediately but he had only a vague recollection of the lady standing there waving to him.

It was his mother, but August was in total emotional turmoil. To him, the woman of whom he had such happy memories, and from whom he had such difficulty tearing himself away in Iceland was his mother.

Now that he was back home the whole disturbing process of readjustment would raise its horrendous head once more.

He hadn't been long in the family home in Connaught Avenue, Grimsby, when father and mother realised that they had a problem on their hands. Their son had been to school in Iceland for two years, so all his formal education had been in Icelandic. He seemed to have forgotten all the English he had ever learnt before going away four years before.

August was back in the language and culture cauldron all over again.

Why could they not have left me alone in Iceland where I was happy? he often wondered.

To help him with his English, August was sent to a retired headmaster for private tuition. The pupil relished the one to one nature of these tutorials and learnt rapidly. When he reckoned that August had pulled up to a suitable level his coach recommended that he be sent to the local Elementary School at the commencement of the autumn term.

His introduction to school in England proved to be quite a shock for the new pupil. Nunsthorpe Elementary was situated in one of the roughest areas of Grimsby. Boys had to be tough to survive in that environment.

Changing schools can be an unsettling experience for any pupil at any age, or stage of education, but when the latest addition to Nunthorpe Elementary made his appearance in the playground he didn't stand a chance.

There was the name for a start.

August Ebenezersson.

The few bullies who could manage to articulate the new boy's strange name laughed at it. And the others stumbled over it, made vain and half-hearted attempts to pronounce it, then laughed because they couldn't say it at all!

Then there were the clothes.

Mother Gwen probably thought that her son looked a picture setting out that first morning. He was all dressed up in his finest white Icelandic sweater with navy blue birds sweeping across the front of it in full flight. His short trousers failed to conceal the stout rubber garters whose job it was to hold up the thick woollen stockings which granny in Iceland had knit especially for the occasion. A pair of shiny but creaky black ankle boots served to complete the unusual back-to school outfit.

If mother thought he looked well, his classmates certainly didn't. For the first three months at Nunsthorpe they teased him mercilessly. They mocked his name, tweaked his garters and using elaborate and exaggerated arm movements bombed about the playground like navy blue birds.

In such a circumstance the bullied boy had only two avenues of action open to him. He could succumb and be bullied for the rest of his days. Or he could hit out and fight back.

August Ebenezersson was of steely Viking stock, and he chose the latter option.

Those who mocked him were mocked back and anybody who dared come close enough with malicious intent was treated to a full-blooded slap, or punch, or kick.

When August was in his second year in Nunthorpe, his teacher, Miss Williamson brought a new boy to sit beside him. She knew that August had experienced the upheaval of settling in to a different school, mid-stream in his education, and assumed he would be an ideal mentor for someone in the same position.

Michael Lee's family had moved in just around the corner from Connaught Avenue, and the two boys became firm friends almost at once. It wasn't long until they felt as much at home in each other's houses as they did in their own, and from the first time August met Michael's mum he was extremely envious of his friend.

Mrs. Lee was a lovely woman. She was kind and understanding and always spoke with a gentle authority that appealed to him. Nothing ever seemed too much trouble to her and she always appeared to have limitless time to listen to the dreams and schemes of two ten year-old schoolboys.

What August didn't realise at the time was that he had for the first time in his life come across a really genuine Christian. He had often heard stories about Jesus in Religious Instruction in School and he used to imagine that He would be something like Mrs. Lee.

Her influence didn't rub off on her son's best friend, unfortunately.

It was still the survival of the fittest as far as August was concerned and he was surviving admirably. By the end of that second year at school he not only commanded respect among his peers, but he had also acquired a reputation.

One day when Kristin's husband, Denys, who was an officer and a gentleman, saw the mad young man whom he had inherited for a brother-in-law giving a playmate a pounding in the back garden he was appalled. August's capacity to curse was as bad as anything he had ever heard in the forces. He had exploded into expletives before launching one particularly savage attack.

Denys was disgusted. Turning to his father-in-law he said, "That is an animal you have growing up out there, and he will become worse if he stays around here. You ought to send him to Cheam in Surrey. I know the Headmaster and I can vouch for the School. You can be assured that he will be both well taught and firmly disciplined there."

August's father liked the idea and at the commencement of the next school year the twelve-year-old lad was packed off to Cheam to be prepared for the Common Entrance Examination for Repton Public School in Derbyshire.

The move may have at least temporarily controlled young August's fiery temper but it didn't guarantee him immunity from bullying. He was back on the merry-go-round again. Older boys from wealthy backgrounds ridiculed the son of a trawler skipper in his way-out clothes. It was a case of having to establish himself once again.

Although he didn't emerge as an A-star pupil in the entrance examination August was granted entry to the famous old school, not so much on his own academic performance, but by virtue of his brother's sporting prowess.

When brother Rabbee was at Repton he had been a member of both the football and hockey first teams. Chess was a favourite pastime of the Icelandic people and big brother was also respected as a former School chess champion.

August followed in Rabbee's footsteps and represented the school in football, hockey and shooting. He may not have been as successful as some in more academic pursuits, but his sporting ability was widely recognised.

In the summer holidays of 1951 a friend of the family arranged for the up-and-coming sportsman to join Grimsby Town

Football Club for their pre-season training programme. The manager of the day, Bill Shankley, spared no mercy in putting the promising young player through his paces with the first team squad. As a result August returned to Repton at the start of the autumn term fitter than he had ever been. He was all fired up and ready to go. It seemed as though he would be assured of a place in the first team, and possibly even a career in sport.

Then tragedy struck again.

In the second match he was forced to retire in pain with what appeared to be little more than a pulled thigh muscle. The injury didn't heal sufficiently for him to resume his place on the team or even the training ground, however.

Having battled through a sense of rejection when evacuated to Iceland at four, the taunts of bullyboys twice, at both eight and then twelve, he was now faced with another deep disappointment.

It was discovered that the aspiring sportsman had a debilitating condition with a very daunting name. It was ankylosingspondulitis.

August Ebenezersson would never play football again.

He was sidelined at sixteen.

THE BLACKNESS OF DARKNESS

2

August felt bitter, and betrayed by life. He had been happy to endure the rigorous training programme at Grimsby Football Club for he was convinced that it would help him achieve a teenager's pipedream. His secret ambition was to go to Cambridge University and wear the famous pale blue shirt at soccer.

That was never now going to be and with his dream dashed to pieces August lashed back at life. He reacted angrily and rapidly became a Repton rebel.

If there was any anti-establishment activity to be engaged in, August was at it. He soon became recognised as a ringleader of revolt. His subconscious assertive sense was determined to have him noticed, one way or another.

August Ebenezersson began to smoke and drink, both of which were totally forbidden under the stringent rules of post-war Repton. Visits to the headmaster's office became more frequent. The beatings, which were designed to cure the rebel of behaviour so unbefitting to a young gentleman in the making, became more severe. And with every visit the Headmaster began to sound more convincing when making his 'definitely your last chance' threats of expulsion.

When he did leave school at seventeen and a half, not having distinguished himself in any way, August was articled to a firm of accountants in Lincoln. Maths had always been one of his better subjects at school but the work in an accountant's office didn't appeal to him. The lively teenager didn't fancy spending the rest of his life cooped up in an office being confronted with columns of figures. Imagining that life in the capital would have more to offer he ran away to London after eighteen months.

It didn't prove as easy to find employment there as he had assumed it would be. When asked about his schooling August presumed that the very mention of the name of a well-known public school would be beneficial. What he feared, though, was any prospective employer contacting the school for he hadn't exactly covered himself with glory there!

While in the process of making a number of ultimately fruitless job applications August discovered the Public Schools Appointment Bureau, an organisation specialising in placing former students in employment. He made himself known to them, and when they had assessed his experience and capabilities they gave him the addresses of six firms to contact.

The first of these to respond was James Beattie Ltd. of Wolverhampton, a large department store. August travelled across the country for an interview with them, and was appointed as a management trainee.

He had just commenced work in his new position for a few weeks when his boss came to him with an unusual request.

"August," he began, with a smile, "this surname of yours is giving us trouble, not only to pronounce, but also to spell. It is also rather cumbersome for customers. Is there any chance that you could change it to something more manageable?"

The new employee promised to consider the possibility. If I do change my name, he mused, it will have to be to something of a Nordic nature. I cannot disown my Icelandic ancestry.

He considered the matter for a few days and then came up with the answer. A few months previously he had been reading Nicholas Monserrat's maritime novel, 'The Cruel Sea', and the exploits of the hero, Captain Ericson were still fresh in his mind. He would change his name to Ericson. It would be an ideal replacement, for it began and ended like an Ebenezersson, while dispensing with the muddle in the middle.

His employers were pleased at this, the customers were happier with it, and August Ericson had embarked upon a career in retailing.

Although he was working in the West Midlands, August's heart was back in Lincolnshire, and in September 1956 he married his childhood sweetheart, Gillian, in St. James' Church, Grimsby. Since Gillian had won a number of local beauty contests, the wedding attracted a certain media attention and photographs appeared in many of the newspapers in the area.

The newly wed couple moved to live in Wolverhampton and a baby daughter, Camilla, was born. Cracks began to appear in the marriage and after a few unsettled years the couple returned to their native Grimsby, where August secured a job as an advertising salesman. Nothing seemed to improve on the home front, however, and sadly the marriage was destined to end in divorce.

August was deeply distressed. Gillian had moved back to live with her parents, taking baby Camilla, who had been the light of both their lives, with her.

He felt isolated again. He was alone in the world, once more. Depression set in.

There were times when he considered ending it all. An overdose of tablets or a short, sharp shot would put him out of his misery. And who would care if he did?

Nobody, he reckoned.

Those were dark, desperate, desolate days.

Chinks of light began to pierce the persistent blackness that seemed to surround him when he met another girl, six months after the breakdown of his marriage.

Perhaps there was hope for him yet.

Could happiness still be just around the corner?

After a few social contacts with his new friend, August decided to become more serious about the relationship, if possible, and so he invited her to meet him for a meal. Having made his 'date' for a Saturday evening August looked forward to it for some time.

The gloom was lifting. A new lady in his life would give him a fresh interest in living. Would October 22, 1966, be the night that would change his life forever?

He spent some time in preparation for that evening and left home in ample time to be early at the restaurant where they had agreed to meet.

August was on the last phase of his journey, and was making a right turn off a main road into a side street, with his indicator flashing, when there was a sudden sickening crunch of crumpling metal. He had been hit broadside by a speeding car full of celebrating students.

The force of the impact drove August right across the front of the car. He ended up in the passenger seat with his back against the front-seat passenger door but his right foot didn't seem to have followed him. It was trapped in a tangle of twisted metal between the accelerator and brake pedals. It seemed so far away and so detached, as though it had been unhitched from him somehow.

'My leg is off', was the single thought that forced its way into and around his anguished brain. 'But it won't matter. Sure I'm going to die anyway…'

Then he passed out.

He was back to the bleakness of the blackness of darkness.

A FULL SPIKER

3

When he regained consciousness August was still trapped in the wreck that had once been his car. He was in excruciating pain.

There was a lot of noise and confusion but all that registered with him were the soothing voices of a lady who had rushed out from a nearby property and a motorcycle policeman. They seemed to be taking it in turns to assure him that the ambulance was on its way.

Although it appeared like an age of anguish to him, the ambulance arrived in a very short time. Then came the almost unbearable agony of the transfer from the compressed car to the waiting ambulance. Searing pain shot like electric shocks though every bone, joint and limb of his body. There was blood splattered all over August's thoughtfully chosen night-out clothes.

On arrival at the Hospital the paramedics wheeled the accident victim into a recovery room on a trolley, made him as comfortable as they could and left. This latest patient had the misfortune to make his appearance just as the day staff were signing off from the Casualty department, and the night staff were coming on for their usually extremely busy Saturday night shift.

He felt, not for the first time in his life, alone and isolated. Now, though, August could add physical agony to all the mental and emotional anguish that had become part of his everyday life.

The overall pain was so intense that he was almost delirious.

After ten or fifteen minutes, which felt more like two or three hours to the mangled man on the trolley, the door opened and the night sister walked in, to check on the latest arrival. In her freshly pressed navy uniform and white frilled cap she appeared as an angel of light to him. Her broad smile brought him an immediate sense of reassurance and comfort. If anybody is going to help me, it will be her, he realised immediately.

The sister crossed to his trolley, spoke soothingly to him, and having assessed the nature and extent of his injuries arranged for him to be transferred to a hospital bed.

Two housemen came to August's bedside, examined him and said that they would have to prepare him for skin traction. He had felt confident in the care of the sister, but August felt decidedly uneasy with these two junior doctors. They were both foreign nationals neither of whom had been in Britain very long and their command of English wasn't particularly good.

The shattered right leg had to be shaved in preparation for the application of the Thomas's splint. This meant a further session of mind-numbing pain.

As the weary hours of that nightmare night ticked slowly through towards morning the sister came several times to the bedside to try and ease August's pain and offer words of encouragement. On one occasion she escorted some of his concerned relatives into the ward and then stood beside them, speaking to them and the new admission, time about.

Next morning when the charge nurse of the orthopaedic ward came on duty he was horrified. He took one look at August and exclaimed, "Who on earth did this?!" The inexperienced housemen had put on a splint that was too small and had used the wrong form of traction. This combination had caused an exacerbation, rather than a relief of the patient's pain. The orthopaedic nurse changed the splint immediately and this brought an easing of the agony.

Before he could have surgery to reset his damaged leg August contracted pneumonia resulting from the trauma of the accident. This meant that he could not be given an anaesthetic to manipulate the bones into place and so surgery had to be delayed.

August was moved into a section of the ward nicknamed Kettle's Corner after the local undertakers, and there he stayed until he was considered out of danger and his leg was set. He was then placed in traction once more. After having been closely monitored for a few days following his surgery he was returned to the long stay ward as it was anticipated that his splintered leg would take some time to heal.

The men in the orthopaedic ward were a lively bunch. Few of them were seriously ill but all of them were forced to remain in hospital as they bad been immobilised by a variety of physical restrictions. Days rolling into weeks in each other's company had the effect of taking a number of individual patients with ailing bodies but active minds and forging them into a fraternity of fun. They played practical jokes on each other, on their visitors, and on as many of the nursing staff as they knew would enter into the spirit of it.

One Saturday night, much to August's delight, the sister who had been so kind to him on the night that he had been admitted, came on duty on the ward. He hadn't seen her for weeks and when she reappeared she had the same effect on him as she had on that first frightful, eventful evening. She appeared to him as an angel of light, a messenger of mercy from some distant peaceful planet.

The sister began her night on duty by doing a ward round, stopping and chatting at every bed. As August saw her move slowly past the beds and heard her laugh heartily at some of the comments of the other patients he felt a warm glow rise up within him.

I wonder will she spend as much time with me as she is doing with some of those other guys? he began asking himself. It was strange. An entire rota of nursing staff had come and gone for days and nights over the weeks. Some had been kind and considerate and had entered into the life of the ward, while others were efficient and businesslike with no time for frivolity.

To August this one was a class apart from any of them. There was something indescribably appealing about her.

His heart gave an involuntary flutter as she came over to the side of his bed with a sheaf of papers in her hands, and began to speak to him. She recalled the night that he had been admitted and August described to her, in more minute detail than was necessary, all that had happened since then. Jill, as she had told him to call her, could probably have read far more about it than he knew in the notes she was carrying but it was important to keep her near him for as long as possible!

She had to move on though, and August's admiring eyes followed her until she had spoken to every patient and left the ward. Sometime between two and three in the morning she returned to do a 'ghost' round to check that everyone was settled and asleep. Most of the other men were sleeping soundly, but August wasn't. When Sister Jill spotted that he was still awake she asked in a gentle whisper, "Would you like a cup of tea?"

She made it sound as though the most important thing in the world that she would like to do at that moment was make him a cup of tea.

"I certainly would," August whispered in reply. In less than fifteen minutes she was back by his side with the promised cup of tea and a biscuit by way of a bonus. Another muted conversation, skilfully stretched out by the man in the bed, ensued.

That was the first of a number of long conversations between nurse and patient when Jill came on to do her weekend night duty.

Planning those encounters became an important part of August's meditative hours. The anticipated advent of his angel at the weekend helped him pass the long hours during the week.

Within a month August began to admit to himself what the men in the beds all around him already knew. They could read it in his eyes, his smile, and his tone of voice. He was falling head over heels in love with the Saturday night sister.

There could be no disguising it. He had to let Jill know how he felt so he wrote her a letter in which he had enclosed some poetry. Then one Saturday night he passed it to her after his middle of the night cup of tea.

Jill replied in a letter that came through the post to the hospital ward the next week. August was thrilled to read of the confession she felt compelled to make. As a professional on duty she had to keep a tight rein on her emotions, but in truth she felt exactly the same way about him as he did about her. The feeling was mutual.

They agreed to keep writing to each other but as they began to express their love more openly through the mail, which had begun to increase, not only in intensity but also in frequency, Jill found herself in a dilemma. She knew that she couldn't carry on nursing in the ward, feeling as she did about one of the patients, and so she requested a transfer to another hospital. This was granted and Jill disappeared from August's ward, but not from his life.

This left him depending solely on the visits of his family and Rev. Stephen Phillips, the hospital chaplain and curate of St. James' Church, Grimsby. Stephen portrayed Christian love and concern for all in the ward and August felt an attraction to him that he could not explain.

God had entered his life again.

In late February 1967, when the specialists considered that August's traction would have performed its function and that his leg should have healed sufficiently, it was removed. This was a great relief to him, but the respite was to be alarmingly short-lived.

Later that day as he was leaning forward in the bed to have his back washed there was a resounding crack. It was such a sickening sound that the man in the next bed fainted.

August's right leg had re-fractured.

When the orderly who had been helping him with his ablutions called the sister on duty she could scarcely credit it.

"It can't be broken again!" she exclaimed in disbelief.

"Well I can tell you that it is," August replied wryly. He knew, for he was in agony again, and back to square one.

This unexpected and unwelcome development required more than four hours of major bone graft surgery to repair. When it was complete August was encased in plaster of Paris from the neck to the point of the toe on the leg on which the operation had been performed. He could only move his arms and his left leg.

The staff who had fitted his plaster cast informed him that he was one of very few people to have been given what they termed 'a full spiker'. As spring gave way to summer and the days became longer and warmer August reckoned that to have been accorded the honour of 'a full spiker' was a rather dubious privilege!

Life became laborious.

It was hard to be a patient patient with a body that looked like the shell of some great white beetle and a mind that was constantly awhirl. He became so disgruntled that the hospital authorities moved the motionless troublemaker to an annexe where his attitude would have a less detrimental effect upon all around him.

August began to look forward increasingly to the days when Jill came to see him. She came regularly on her bicycle and her visits were like rays of the summer sunshine outside flooding the ward. It was only her positive approach that helped him come to terms, in at least some measure, with the limitations imposed by the 'full spiker'.

In his calmer moments he often looked back to that night almost a year before. He had set out to meet one woman and had ended up in hospital where he had met another for the very first time, in totally unforeseen circumstances.

Jill is a wonderful woman, he would remind himself repeatedly in the cosy afterglow of one of her visits. Do I not deserve her though? he would continue to muse ruefully. Have I not suffered enough to merit her attention?

Those were the substance of his more placid reveries, and for Jill's sake and with her encouragement, he began to try and move around with the aid of crutches. He found it an unbelievably tortuous experience, however.

Most of the time he just kept fuming away furiously, "When am I ever going to be out of this place? And out of THIS THING?"

VICTORIA

4 Despite the spiker August had mastered the art of mobility sufficiently, with the aid of crutches, to be discharged from hospital by early November.

If he had felt imprisoned in his full-length plaster cast in the hospital, the prospects of living a normal life were not enormously enhanced by his return home. His father had died and his mother was living in a flat on the top floor of a high-rise development in Grimsby. His daily routine alternated between lying in the bed, lying on the bed, or lying around in the living room. As with life in the hospital, so it was with life in the flat. The sole highlights of an otherwise monotonous existence were Jill's regular visits. She came often on her bicycle bringing snippets of news from the local community and an optimistic outlook which helped furnish August with hope for the future. He had been at home for little more than a month when, on one of his check-up visits to the Hospital, the doctors decided that it was time to remove the spiker and replace it with a calliper splint. Although it still impaired his movement to some degree, the calliper meant that he could now sit up, rather that having to lie down most of the time. What a marvellous relief that was!

With a fully active mind and a now semi-functional body August wanted to return to work. He had been lying in and around hospitals for more than a year and had followed business trends as far as possible from the local newspapers and TV reports. He longed to make a come back in the world of retailing. The question was though, what company would want a half-crocked former buyer and salesman who had been out of the marketplace for almost fifteen months, to spearhead their sales initiative?

August applied for a number of jobs.

Thanks for your application, came the reply, but our post is demanding, and would require full fitness.

August contacted a number of former employers.

We appreciate your wealth of experience, they told him, but we don't have any vacancies just at the moment. Get in touch again when you are fully recovered.

It was frustrating.

Every rebuff just served to make August all the more resolute.

He wanted employment. He needed employment. But what he needed more than anything was an employer who was desperate.

Just before Christmas he found one. And they were delighted to find him.

The Scunthorpe Co-op had lost their former manager just over a week before Christmas. It was the busiest time of year for almost any business and August was employed and helped steer them through into the New Year. He had learnt to walk fairly well with the aid of a stick by then, and the psychological boost of feeling both wanted and worthwhile aided his recovery immensely.

There was a second factor that helped him readjust to the routine of everyday life even more than his return to a career in retailing, and that was his marriage to Jill. As their meetings became more frequent, and their relationship more meaningful, August and Jill realized that they wanted to spend the remainder of their lives together. They felt so much at home in each other's company.

The wedding, in the registry office in Scunthorpe in January 1968, was a low-key affair. There was none of the paparazzi attention of August's earlier marriage. Jill had a daughter, Jane, who lived with her, and was the child of a former marriage, and August had a daughter, Camilla, who didn't live with him, and was the child of a former marriage, so neither bride nor groom felt the need for anything more than a simple ceremony.

Then in the autumn of 1968, two significant events occurred in the life of August Ericson. The first was that he became a father again, for Jill and he were thrilled to welcome their baby son Timothy into the world. In contrast to the joy that their new little boy brought into their lives, August's appointment as regional manager of the Co-op in South Wales presented them with the prospect of the upheaval of moving house.

They did this quite happily, however, and by Christmas, when August had completed a year back at work the little family was safely settled in Wales.

In August 1970 Jill went into hospital for the birth of her second child, but there were complications. Following a prolonged labour the new baby was found to be experiencing difficulty in breathing and oxygen was administered.

As little Victoria began to grow she seemed to scream all the time. At the beginning August and Jill thought that she was merely a restless baby and would 'settle down' as she matured.

When the situation failed to improve, Jill, with a combination of nursing experience and maternal instinct, began to suspect that there was something more serious the matter with their little one. When just a few months old she started to take short fits, which were worrying to watch, and as she grew older these developed into more distressing convulsions. It was discovered that Victoria was severely handicapped, both physically and mentally. She continued to scream almost ceaselessly unless carried around and stimulated.

It was hard for the parents.

Timothy was a toddler walking around, investigating everything with a childish curiosity. He required watching for most of his waking hours. That became a problem, for his little sister Victoria was demanding his parents attention all of the time, for she had little else but waking hours, most of which she spent crying.

August and Jill loved her dearly but they were often at their wit's end to know how to cope.

There were times when August couldn't even entertain the thought of going home, especially after a trying day at work. On such occasions he went out for a drink with some of his workmates, arriving home just in time to go to bed.

In spite of these periodic demonstrations of selfishness by her increasingly hassled husband, Jill continued to manage the children, including Victoria with all her needs, day by day. Her daughter Jane, who was ten years old, showed a special love for, and capacity for working with, her little half-sister, and was a tremendous help to her mum.

Baby Victoria needed constant care and eventually her parents decided to return to Lincolnshire to be near to both their families. At least when there they wouldn't feel as cut-off as in Cardiff, and Jill could call on the support of her relatives during some of the more demanding days.

With such a move in prospect August began job-hunting again and secured a position in Mawer and Collingham's, a privately owned department store in Lincoln. He was content to take a post offering less salary than he had been earning in Cardiff, for money had ceased to be the uppermost matter in his mind at that time.

Victoria was his main concern.

Her condition and care had become the chief priority.

Everyone loved little vexed Victoria, and if they could see her happy, they would be happy.

A PATENT INNER PEACE

5   Although Victoria still required round-the-clock
care and attention, when the family returned to their
native Lincolnshire help was at hand, and August
soon settled into his new position as buyer in the men's department
of Mawer and Collingham.

The staff with whom he worked were all charming,
considerate, and very good salesmen. The company operated a
discounting policy to the customer and this was matched by a
commission incentive to the sales staff. In order to maintain a brisk
turnover of stock, any suit that had been on the hanger for more
than twelve months was offered for sale at a very reasonable price
and the salesman making the sale was given a commission.

There was one member of the counter staff who seemed to
benefit regularly from this inducement, and there was also something
about this particular man that appealed to the clothing buyer. His
transparent honesty was often remarked upon, and occasionally even
somewhat resented, by others who were inclined to take short cuts
with the truth.

August liked him, though. This man reminded him, in some
strange way, of his friend Michael's mum from his childhood days.

He seemed to live his life, as she had done, in a constant state of composure. Nothing appeared to faze him, nothing was ever too much trouble for him and everybody, whoever they were, or whatever their problem, mattered to him.

One evening, when most of the other staff had gone, August was conscious that he had waited behind to speak to him.

"I hope you don't mind me troubling you, August," he began, " but I have something to ask you. Perhaps it is more of a suggestion to put to you."

"Yes," August replied, puzzled, " and what is that?" He had no idea what was coming, but he knew that whatever it was would be worth stopping in his step to hear, if it came from that particular person.

"I go to a Baptist Church and my friend Dick Hardy, who is a postman during the week is also our pastor. Dick believes God has given him a special ministry in praying for the sick. He has done this on a number of occasions recently and some of the people have been healed."

The salesman paused before continuing with his question suggestion.

"We have been concerned about little Victoria and all that you have told us about her. Would you mind if Dick came to your home and prayed for her sometime?" he asked.

"No, I wouldn't mind at all," August replied. "Jill and I would be glad to see him anytime." They would be grateful for anything that could prove helpful. August reckoned, too, that even if somebody praying for Victoria, whatever that entailed, didn't do their little daughter any good, it certainly couldn't do her much harm.

A date and time were duly arranged and Dick came to call at their home. He was another one of these friendly, focused and ever-so-sincere kind of people. Dick sat and chatted to them over a cup of tea, gaining an instant entrance into their hearts by talking to them about the subject nearest to those hearts, their children. He heard of the kindness of Jane, the antics of toddler Timothy, and the web of love and longing that was being woven around baby Victoria with all her apparent handicaps.

When he considered it appropriate Dick indicated that he was going to pray for Victoria. He crossed to where she was lying and placed his hands gently on her head before anointing her with oil and praying that God would heal her, and that He would reveal Himself in a special way to her parents, Jill and August.

After having prayed, Dick didn't sit down again. He talked to the parents on his way to the door, and then bade them both a warm 'Goodbye' and left.

A few minutes later, when they had returned to the side of the cot containing Victoria, Jill remarked, "There was something different about that man. I just can't put my finger on it, but he appeared so calm and confident. It was as though he was totally committed to whatever it is he believes in. Whether it does Victoria any good though, we will have to wait and see."

August agreed with her. Dick was certainly different.

This was the third one of these people that he had come across at close quarters, and Jill's remarks set him thinking.

Why are these people so different? How can they have such a patent inner peace? Is it something to do with the fact that they are all religious types? It must be, for they do a lot of talking about God, and that man Dick actually talked *to* Him as though he knew Him.

It would be great, he concluded, if I could be like that.

I would love to see my life surrounded by the serenity that they seem to know.

Will I ever meet Dick, or any more of these people again?

And will God reveal Himself to me in some special way?

If He will, how will He?

Thoughts like these continued to flit across his mind from time to time but August could never afford the time to give them any more than a cursory consideration.

There were other things to think about as well.

He had been promoted to senior manager status within Mawer and Collingham's, and so his business commitments occupied a major part of his week. His chief concern, though, was the one he came home to every evening, and left behind him at home every morning.

It was the welfare of Victoria.

As she had grown older her needs had increased both in intensity and complexity, and so her continued care had become more of a responsibility.

Jill found that despite the efforts of family and friends to help, the constant demands upon her attention were beginning to sap her strength and prey on her mind. She needed some sort of relief, and her infant daughter needed specialist treatment.

Thus when Victoria was just a year old, her totally devoted, but often disconsolate parents were delighted to discover that there was a hospital unit specialising in the care of the severely handicapped in Caistor, eighteen miles from Lincoln.

They made an appointment at the hospital and the staff in the children's unit conducted a thorough assessment of Victoria's condition and arranged a series of interviews with Jill and August. On the basis of their finings they offered to take the little girl into the unit for the weekend, every weekend from then on.

This proved to be a blessing to all three parties concerned.

The hard-pressed parents were able to relax with each other for the first time in over a year, and also spend time with their other two children, Jane and Timothy. Jill especially often felt pangs of conscience that she hadn't the same time to devote to Victoria's older brother and sister as she was compelled to spend with her. She took heart, though, from the fact that neither Jane nor Timothy ever complained of their lot.

In the children's unit in the hospital the very able charge nurse was conducting pioneering research into the care of the severely mentally handicapped and he was delighted to have Victoria coming in every weekend. He had never treated anyone so young before and her visits afforded him the opportunity to embark upon groundbreaking study as he monitored both her condition and her treatment.

The most significant benefit of all was to Victoria herself. As she began to respond to the treatment she was being given Victoria's mum and dad noticed tremendous strides of improvement both in her condition and her behaviour. She seemed to spend less time in tears of frustration, but rather she started to react positively to certain stimuli. This encouraged Jane and Timothy for they began to gain pleasure from being in her presence and attempting to play with her.

At last Victoria had become a fully-fledged member of the family.

Then in September 1972, when Victoria was just over two and beginning to be a source of delight rather than a cause for concern to all around her, tragedy struck. She contracted a chest infection, and when she went into hospital one weekend the staff were worried about her condition and kept her in.

Within a few days, despite expert nursing care, she had passed away.

The family was devastated. Just when the little one had started to recognise them and contribute to their collective happiness she was taken from them.

God had chosen not to heal her in any gradual physical sense. Rather, He had elected to take her home to be with Himself in heaven, where a complete and immediate transformation could be effected.

Jill and August received many messages of condolence during those dark days of grief and loss, and the senior manager at Mawer and Collingham's was touched by the sympathy shown to him by the large staff. The salesman who had arranged for Dick to come and pray for Victoria was amongst the first to express his condolences. Others followed. Wherever he went as he moved about in the store someone was sure to stop him to sympathise.

Two weeks after the funeral had taken place August sent a memo to all the staff thanking them for their support during a very difficult period, but saying that it was now time to move on.

This was how both Jill and he felt.

They had their own personal happy memories of Victoria, but realised that they should now concentrate on making life as productive as possible for Jane and Timothy, and looking forward to the new baby which Jill was expecting in December. And beyond that their lives stretched out ahead of them towards a dim and undefined horizon.

Dick had prayed that God would heal Victoria and reveal Himself in a special way to her parents.

The first phase of that prayer had been answered. God had healed Victoria in a total, if perhaps unexpected, fashion.

The second was still awaiting His attention.

MORE QUESTIONS THAN ANSWERS

6

The trauma of Victoria's death was alleviated for all four family members by the birth of baby Emma just three months later, on December 21, 1972. Now August and Jill, Jane and Timothy had another little bundle on which to lavish the affection once showered upon Victoria.

August continued to work hard and progress up the management ladder at Mawer and Collingham's, and on Emma's second birthday, in December 1974, the family moved into what for them was a dream home on the outskirts of Lincoln.

It seemed that they had everything that anyone could wish for now. Their new home had a luxury fitted kitchen and built-in furniture in all the bedrooms. The entire house was double-glazed at a time when double-glazing was the exception rather than the rule. A Ford Granada graced the sweeping drive at the front of the house, with the compliments of the company.

The Ericsons never had it so good. Or at least so it appeared to all who knew them. Gradually, too, they began to ease themselves into a social circle of professional people. August began collecting antiques and fine china, and became a connoisseur of fine wine.

He embarked upon a number of very profitable ventures for the company and was rewarded accordingly. Soon August was in charge of all twelve buyers in a large department store in which staff and management had a cordial but effective working relationship.

As he became accepted into a new round of social engagements with his ever expanding body of friends, many of whom were intellectual types, he found himself becoming engaged in deep and meaningful discussions with them, often far into the night. The company might vary according to the nature of the occasion or the location of the event, but when August was around the subject seldom did.

It was always something to do with the meaning of life. What, he was anxious to know, was the point of it all? As an avid student of history August could cite examples of great men who had accomplished marvellous things in their lifetimes but had ended their lives in isolation and misery. Is there any point or purpose, or any joy or justice in anything? was the gist of his constant query.

By this time his position in the company was secure and it appeared that he had a job for life. His career was like a railway line stretching out in front of him. He knew where all the stations were and he could stop there for refuelling along the way. At one he would become a managing director and from there it would be an easy downhill gradient to his final destination. When he slackened speed to glide into the buffers at the terminus he would prepare himself for the grand reception on the last platform of life. That would be a big retirement evening with an engraved watch, a substantial lump sum by way of a bonus and the promise of a comfortable pension for the years to come. He could then enjoy the sunset years of his life in the siding of retirement, indulging in just about anything that took his fancy.

All that remained for him to do was stay on the rails and enjoy the view as he listened to the clackety-clack of the years rolling past.

It all seemed so cosy and so comfortable but yet for some reason that he found himself struggling to explain, August was neither cosy nor comfortable with the prospect of it. It didn't matter whether he was driving his powerful car, sitting in his air-conditioned office or relaxing in his well-appointed home, the same question kept cropping up in his mind, time and time again.

Is this all there is to life? it persisted. Is this IT?

Occasionally he would remonstrate with himself. Ninety-five percent of the world's population would envy you your lifestyle, he concluded, in his more appreciative, reflective moments. And what's more they would be shocked to learn that you weren't one hundred per cent happy.

There were times when August thought long and hard about his role as a member of society. Could the sense of emptiness that seemed to be swelling like a balloon being blown up to fill the whole inside of him be related to the fact that he didn't have a job that was of significant value to others?

Take my father, for instance, he mused more than once. His life had been worthwhile. He had gone to sea as a trawler skipper, in all weathers, to bring back fish to feed the people. This contribution had been particularly important during the war when people's lives had depended on his capacity to land fish.

Doctors and nurses, too, teachers and policemen, they all did something, somehow to make life more pleasant, or at least more bearable, for somebody. What, though, was he? A man who moved STUFF from place to place in an effort to make money for his employers, so that they in turn could pass some of it on to him. This was designed to motivate him to such an extent that he would move even more STUFF from place to place so that he could make even more money for his employers so that they in turn could pass it on to him so that he could…

He was like a hamster on a wheel in a shiny sterile cage. He had an endless supply of food and water, plenty of expensive toys to play with, and always clean shavings on his floor. Yet he spent all day, every day, going round and round on his smooth-running wheel without ever getting anywhere.

In an attempt to achieve some sense of satisfaction August once decided to try and do something to help somebody in need or distress. So he began to look into the question of the alleviation of poverty and suffering across the world and the end result of this was that he became even more frustrated. As he read of starvation, deprivation and exploitation in so-called developing countries he drove himself almost to the point of despair.

There were so many people living out pathetic miserable lives while he lived in relative comfort and yet he seemed powerless to do anything about it. Even the largest contribution he could make to the multitude of charities that seemed to be clamouring for his money, each representing a totally commendable cause, would be like a drop in the ocean when measured up against the magnitude of the problem.

Why were so many people suffering? Why were little children dying of hunger? Why was he so useless, so helpless, so empty and so unfulfilled?

He appeared to have everything that mattered in life, and yet he had nothing that satisfied in life. Surely there must be more to living than this brand of outwardly prosperous but substantially unproductive existence.

August's mind was forced to admit another dimension to his reasoning on the value and meaning of life in general, and his own in particular over the Easter weekend in 1979.

On Good Friday night the Ericson family had gathered around the TV to spend a relaxing evening watching the Lew Grade production of 'Jesus of Nazareth', starring Robert Powell in the title role.

Early education in an Anglican Public School had served to furnish August with nothing more than a nodding acquaintance with the story of Jesus. He had, with all his other classmates, sung carols at Christmas, drawn crosses and chickens at Easter, and heard some of the stories that Jesus had told recounted with varying degrees of enthusiasm throughout the year. Two of these stood out in his mind. One was about a farmer sowing seed in all different types of soil and the other was the story of a young man who had left home with a fortune, to try and make a fortune, and had ended up coming back home to his father broken and bankrupt.

His general perception of the story of Jesus had always remained one of injustice. It had always seemed singularly spiteful to him that the Jewish nation should so despise, and eventually sentence to death one of its own people. Why should they want to kill somebody whose sole desire was to teach his particular dogma of love and peace and heal afflicted people as a miracle-working philanthropist?

The early part of the film held August spellbound. There was something mysteriously captivating about the portrayal of Jesus as He was baptised by John in the Jordan, called His disciples by the Sea of Galilee and taught His doctrine and healed the sick in the towns and on the hillsides of Judaea.

As the film rolled on into its second hour, however, and it became obvious from the scene of Judas' treacherous betrayal of his master in the Garden of Gethsemane that things were about to take an ugly and violent turn August became increasingly uncomfortable. He wanted to cry out in protest and yet his soft side was crying inwardly out of a sense of grief and disbelief.

When it came to the trial scenes, with a frenzied mob yelling out, 'Away with him! Crucify him! We don't want this man to reign over us!' August slipped silently out of the room. He was about to burst into tears and didn't want his family to see him weeping over a film. There was no way that he could bear to watch the visual presentation of the crucifixion. It would be altogether too brutal and too heart-breaking because it seemed so terribly unnecessary and unreasonable.

He stepped outside into the cool spring night and stood in the drive gazing up at the stars. Why had that film upset him so much he began to wonder? Could the life and death of Jesus Christ be related in some way to his constant quest for satisfaction?

Then he began to recall people like Mrs. Lee, Dick Hardy and Stephen Phillips. These three, and one or two others he had met in business from time to time, had talked about Jesus with a strange intimacy that could almost be described as familiarity. It was as though they actually knew Him, and could communicate with Him as a friend. In addition, this relationship, or whatever it was, must have equipped them with a steadfast serenity for they had all appeared to be unusually settled and satisfied individuals.

How could he find out more about this?

Why did Jesus have to die?

Could anybody who liked come to know Him personally? If the answer to that was 'Yes', then what were the terms and conditions?

It struck August that if he could only learn more about Jesus perhaps he could discover the meaning and purpose of life.

It seemed that he now had more questions than answers.

Where did he begin, though, to find the answers to at least some of his questions?

That in itself was just yet another question!

COLOUR OR BLACK AND WHITE?

7 The questioning continued all summer.

After a few months August had realized that many of his problems could be solved if he could discover the answer to just two questions. These were basically, how can I know peace and purpose in my life, and if I were to find out more about Jesus Christ, would that help?

He decided to ask the Wedmores. Keith Wedmore was a barrister who had married Jane Collingham, the last remaining member of one of the firm's founding families. August, John Burrows, John Maplethorpe and Brian Buckley sat on the management board of Mawer and Collinghams with them.

August had learnt that Keith and Jane were Quakers. On first hearing this name he wondered if they had shares in a porridge factory as well as the large department store. Further investigation revealed, however, that the Quakers were a minority religious grouping with an unpretentious meeting place in Lincoln.

If he could make contact with the Quakers perhaps they could shed some light on his concerns regarding how to find lasting fulfilment in life.

Company board meetings were usually held in the morning and then at lunchtime the six directors adjourned to the store's restaurant. There they could conclude their business over a specially prepared meal in a less formal atmosphere.

One day when the meal was over and the meeting for the day had finished August spoke to Keith as they put their files and papers in order before leaving the table.

"You will understand that this is a purely personal and private interest, Keith," he began, "but I wonder if you could tell me how I could find out about the Quakers? I would be keen to know something of who they are, and what they believe, that kind of thing."

"That shouldn't be a problem, August," Keith replied at once. "The clerk of the Lincoln meeting is Roger Seal, a schoolteacher. Roger is very well versed in both our history and beliefs. I will give you his phone number, and I will speak to him this afternoon if I can, to let him know you will be calling."

Keith proved as good as his word and when August contacted Roger that evening they arranged to meet later in the week.

August trudged up the hill towards Lincoln Castle on the appointed day, not quite knowing what to expect. Roger had explained to him that his home was called Wayside Cottage, and it was a small house just about two hundreds yards from the historic ancient fortress.

Having followed Roger's directions he found the place without any difficulty. There was no bell, just a heavy brass knocker which seemed to boom all around when August gave it one sharp bang to announce his arrival. Within seconds the heavy door was pulled opened and the schoolmaster Quaker invited August into his simple home.

When he entered the little house it was like stepping off the street straight into a former century. August's immediate impression was that this man must live a very spartan kind of life. There was no

TV in the room, no upholstery on the chairs, and no central heating radiators on the walls. Six or seven chunks of coal, which had been stacked both artistically and scientifically in the centre of a small grate, struggled and spluttered to lay claim to the name of a fire. A large Victorian clock on the polished mantelpiece filled the entire room with its regular, reassuring, re-echoing tick.

August had a momentary mental panic attack. If I become a Quaker, or a follower of Jesus Christ, if that's something different, will I have to sell the lovely home I have worked so hard to procure, and live in stark austerity? he wondered.

Roger's dress code or drinks menu didn't do anything to allay the initial misgivings of his visitor either. The welcoming host was wearing a pair of baggy corduroy trousers, an old-fashioned flannel shirt and a woollen tie with a sloppy shapeless knot. The two side pockets of his coarse Harris Tweed jacket bulged out perceptibly, helping to complete the picture of someone who had all kinds of secrets stored away somewhere, but who was completely disinterested in style and appearance.

Despite his doubts August was intrigued by the ambience of the setting and Roger's rare regalia. He even permitted himself a fleeting smile as he thought, 'this schoolmaster must have escaped from the pages of the pop-up edition of Tom Brown's Schooldays'!

When he had invited August to take a seat, Roger offered his guest some liquid refreshment. "Could I fetch you something to drink?" he enquired. "I have Indian or Chinese tea, lemon barley water or plain water."

August was not surprised that alcoholic beverages were not on offer in such austere surroundings and declined the offer.

"No thank you, I am not long after a meal, " he explained truthfully.

On observing that August had made himself as comfortable as possible on the cushionless wooden armchair to which he had directed him, Roger asked gently, "And what can I do for you?"

There could be no doubting either the warmth of the welcome August was accorded or the simple sincerity of the master of Wayside Cottage.

"I would like to hear about the Quakers, " August replied. "How did your organisation begin, and what do you believe? Indeed I would be interested in anything you can tell me."

"You have come to the right person," Roger remarked in response to his guest's requests. "I have made a lifetime study of our history and beliefs." It was then his turn to afford himself the luxury of a short-lived but satisfied smile.

For the next hour Roger proceeded to tell August how the Quakers had been formed and the fundamentals of their belief. He outlined clearly, kindly, and interspersed with dates which he obviously considered significant, the radical development of the movement. This included numerous references to the impact of leading named Quakers on the social history of England, and the supposed calming influence of the sect on present day society. Roger only stemmed the stream of his discourse to answer his visitor's occasional queries in the search for even more expansive knowledge.

The interview in Wayside Cottage proved to be a most illuminating experience for the inquisitive August. When it came time for him to leave he thanked Roger profusely for taking the time with him, and left for home a much better informed individual. He certainly now had a far clearer picture in his mind of the positive influence of self-effacing religion on the social history of Britain.

On reaching home he spent almost another hour recounting his experiences to Jill. August noticed that his wife appeared more interested in his description of Roger's quaint abode and the contrast between his lifestyle and theirs than she did in the occasional snippets of information he tossed in on the formation and function of the Society of Friends.

As he recalled what he had learnt and paused to reflect on it later in the evening, however, August discovered that he still didn't have the answers to the basic questions which had been plaguing him for months. He hadn't stumbled upon the spring of eternal happiness. Although he had a head full of knowledge he was still left with a horrible hollow at his heart.

When he went to bed that night in late October, 1979, August couldn't sleep. There must be some way out of this mental morass, he kept telling himself.

Then he began to realize that no other human being, however clever, was going to be able to provide him with a satisfactory solution to his problem. The answer must lie at the source of the question, and that was within himself.

Lying there, half-awake but longing to sleep, his whirling mind threw up yet another question for him. It came unexpectedly but with a strange sense of urgency, as though demanding an instant answer.

It was, "Who is Jesus Christ?"

His immediate internal response was both spontaneous and sincere.

"Lord, I believe You are the Son of God and I accept You," he said, and was at once overcome by a peculiar sense of peace. He realised that something momentous had happened but was at a loss to explain it. All he knew was that somehow or other he now belonged to God, for He had accepted him into His family.

He prodded his wife until she grunted sleepily, "What is it, August?"

"Jill, I have accepted Jesus Christ into my life," he told her, struggling to subdue a strange sense of excitement. "But what is more He has accepted me!"

"O.K. O.K. August. Is that all you wanted to tell me?" Jill replied in a faraway detached tone of voice for she was still seventy-five percent asleep. "Go back to sleep."

She then proceeded to take her own advice and return to the blissfully unconscious state from which she had been so rudely roused.

August, though, was very much awake.

It was then that his former life came up before him and he began to confess his sins, as he remembered them, to God. It was as though a disposal skip had been pulled up beside his bed, and as the sins were confessed they disappeared into the depths of it, never to appear again. During those turbulent but rapturous moments August experienced a peculiar mix of spiritual emotions. A realisation of the wretchedness of sin combined with an instinctive awareness that his own sins had been forgiven and the inexplicable joy of having confessed his newly found faith to furnish him with that inner peace he had craved so long. He had arrived at the station of Ultimate Fulfilment long before his journey on the railway of life had been completed. August was only forty-four and reckoned he still had a lot more living to do, and if the joy that he now knew persisted he was going to live life to the full, at last.

His last memory before slipping off into a sound sleep was of putting his hand across the front of his nightshirt to find that it was soaking wet. Tears of contrition had teamed up with tears of joy to leave him a happily exhausted saved soul.

Jill was up first in the morning and as she busied herself around the bedroom August asked from the depths of the sheets, "Tell me, love, did I say anything to you in the middle of the night?"

"Yes, August," his wife replied, in a puzzled tone of voice. It was as though she wasn't sure whether to be amused or afraid. "You mumbled something about Jesus."

"Oh, that's all right. That's *great* in fact," came the even more mystifying response. "It wasn't all a dream then!"

When Jill left the bedroom to go down and organise breakfast for the family August rose from the bed, pulled the curtains and threw open the window. As he gazed down on the garden where just a few straggling summer flowers were trying in vain to prevent the creeping brown of autumn from pervading their remaining petals, August seemed to see everything in a new light. The whole damp garden, which was tinged by the changing hues of dying leaves, seemed to be alive and ablaze with golden life.

It was as though he had spent his whole life up until then watching black and white TV but had been given an unexpected gift of his first colour set!

What he didn't know at that moment was something he was soon to discover.

August Ericson had become a completely new creation in Christ Jesus!

THE BATTERED OLD EXERCISE BOOK

8 When he went downstairs for breakfast August told
his family, who all seemed somehow and suddenly
more precious to him, of his middle of the night
conversion. They were at various stages of dress and preparedness
for going out to work or school when their dad announced, "I had a
wonderful experience last night, kids. I have accepted Jesus Christ
into my life."

There was a short silence during which they all regarded him
strangely. Their dad was into reading history and philosophy, and
occasionally coming off with some highbrow oddball comment on
the meaning of life. This, though, appeared different. He seemed to
be excited, almost ecstatic about it, whatever it was. They had never
seen him quite as enthusiastic about any of his ideas or arguments
before.

Ecstatic was a good word to describe how August felt. Perhaps
euphoric would have been even better. As he drove to work in
Lincoln city centre he saw the world with newly implanted spiritual
vision. What surprised him was that there were so many people
rushing hither and thither to their places of employment yet none
of them seemed as happy as he felt.

Had nobody else in the city ever heard of the liberating power of Jesus Christ?

If they hadn't he would soon let them know!

He hadn't long arrived in work before he began telling his colleagues about his experience of the night before, urging them to trust in Jesus, too, if they wanted to discover satisfaction in their souls.

This went on for days. Everybody August met, whether in the store, on the street or in the neighbourhood where they lived, heard about his dramatic middle of the night encounter with Christ. People edged nervously away when the normally sane and sensible company director began talking about sin, salvation and satisfaction. There were a couple of really weird bits about a skip beside his bed and tears on his nightshirt.

August Ericson had gone funny. Off his head, some said.

Jill couldn't understand it either. Her party-loving husband had completely lost interest in socialising. He appeared to have forfeited all the fun that they once enjoyed in the pubs and clubs with their friends in order to spend time reading an old Bible he had unearthed from somewhere. That was, of course when he wasn't telling somebody else about the joy he had found in Jesus!

When Jill phoned some of their former friends they felt sorry for her.

"That's awful, dear," they would commiserate, in solemn mourning manner, as though there had just been a death in the family. "But don't worry, he will probably get over it. Apparently these religious phases only last a few months and then people return to normal. But you wouldn't think of putting on an appointment for him with a psychiatrist, would you? Just in case, if you know what I mean…?"

While the family and friends were trying to convince one another that the religious bug which had bitten August would soon work its way out of his system, he had a different problem.

Now that he had been transformed by the power of God and born into His heavenly family he longed to meet some of his spiritual brothers and sisters. Surely there must be someone in a city the size of Lincoln, who felt exactly as he did.

Where were they, though?

They certainly hadn't been moving in his social circle for the past ten years.

As he was reflecting on all the people he had ever met who had appeared to be 'far too good to be true' at the time and who had seemed to have a hotline to heaven he remembered Rev. Stephen Phillips. Stephen was the chaplain who had shown him such love, compassion and understanding during his prolonged stay in hospital more than twelve years before. On making enquiries August discovered that Stephen had become vicar of the Anglican Church in Great Limber, the main village on the Earl of Yarborough's estate in northeast Lincolnshire.

August telephoned Stephen, and after reminding him of how they had met in the hospital in Grimsby, told him that he had accepted the Lord Jesus Christ as his Saviour.

There was an immediate, spontaneous "Hallelujah!" from the other end of the phone.

At last August had found somebody who was on the same wavelength as himself. It was comforting to realise that there was at least one other person in Lincolnshire who spoke his language!

It only took Stephen a few minutes to establish that this exuberant new Christian would need some spiritual nurturing so he said, "Why don't you come up and tell me all about it sometime, August? A few of us from the parish here meet for prayer every morning at a quarter to seven. You would be very welcome to join us."

"Thanks for the invitation, Stephen," August was only too happy to reply. "I will be with you tomorrow."

Next morning August was up at four o'clock to read his Bible and then he set off before six, into the murk of an early November morning to drive more than thirty miles to Great Limber. Every mile was a thrill. It would be great to meet others who loved the Lord like he did!

Stephen and his praying friends welcomed August warmly and after the most recent addition to the company had told them of his conversion, they began to pray. What a delight it was to be amongst people who felt at ease in the presence of Almighty God, just bringing the needs of the day before Him!

For months after that, August hardly ever missed an early morning prayer meeting at Great Limber. The sixty five miles round trip was no problem to him. The roads were reasonably clear at that time of the morning and August just praised the Lord as he drove along.

One thing that had intrigued him, right from the very first morning he was there, was the battered old exercise book that Stephen brought with him. Before they would commence he would open it and read out a list of people, or coming events, for which he suggested that they should pray. It could be the name of a church member who was ill, a forthcoming special youth service, or perhaps a wayward son who was the burden of a grieving mother's heart.

As they became more acquainted August expressed an interest in the dog-eared old book with its pencilled entries.

"That book has been on the go a long time, Stephen," he remarked.

"You're right it has," the vicar of Great Limber replied, with a smile. "Many, many years. Wait there until I show you something."

With that he began to scan his way back through the pages, stopping occasionally to nod his head and smile again, as though his discoveries brought back happy memories.

"Ah, here we are," he announced at last with a satisfied sigh. "Look at that, August."

When he looked down at the spot to which Stephen was pointing, August saw, written in pencil on a page with the heading 'November 1966', the name 'August Ericson'.

"Jill's name is in here somewhere, too," Stephen went on to say, and a few more moves up and down an adjacent page with a jerking, searching finger located it.

August fought to keep himself from dropping tears on the page of the battered old book.

"Have you been praying for us since then, Stephen?" August enquired.

"Yes, I have," came the modest reply. "God always answers prayer, August. All He asks of us is that we keep at it. I believe He will bring Jill to Himself as well."

"Praise God!" August exclaimed. "I believe He will too. That's what I am praying for night and day!"

Later on that day, when he and Jill were sitting chatting together August told his wife that their names had been on Stephen's prayer list for years. She was neither as thrilled nor as touched as he had been at his early morning discovery, however.

"Oh have they indeed?" was her off-hand response. "So you have found a soul mate have you, August? Is he as crazy and over the top about religion as you are?"

As the dark days of winter started to close in around her, Jill began to wonder if she could remain with August forever. Should she leave him and go back alone to the life they had once known? The thought crossed her mind more than once.

What kept her with him was the fact that although he had always been a most devoted husband he was now even *more* attentive since his middle of the night, sins in the skip experience. This helped compensate in some measure for the lack of nights out with their friends. It would seem that August had no time for such pursuits now anyway for if he wasn't rushing out to a prayer meeting he was sitting with his nose in his Bible or assuring somebody that he was praying for them, as though this was some special kind of favour!

Looking at, and listening to him, from a purely personal and natural point of view, Jill often wondered if she would want whatever it was that he had. Did she have what it takes to be a sort of visionary religious fanatic? Or had she the stamina to stick the pace?

Her husband sometimes said the strangest things!

One morning on his way back in the car from the early morning prayer session in Great Limber he found that he needed to ring Jill. There had been a lot to pray for that morning and so he had been late in leaving the meeting. He just wouldn't have time to go home as he usually did before going on to work. His wife would be expecting him so it would be important to let her know.

The telephone rang and Jill picked it up.

"Oh hello there, darling'" came August's voice. "I just wanted to tell you that I'm running late and will be going straight on into the store. It was wonderful the way it worked out for I was desperate to ring you and the Lord showed me a telephone box!"

"That's fine, August," Jill replied. "But why did you need *the Lord* to show you a telephone box? Could you not have seen it for yourself?!"

"The Lord, the Lord, the Lord..." she echoed his words in playful mimicry while walking away after having replaced the receiver. "It seems as if my August can't do anything now without the Lord!"

Little did she know it, but she was right!

The Lord had become the hub of her husband's life.

All that August wanted to do was love and serve Him, every minute of every day! And he still yearned to meet with others who loved Him too.

Stephen had advised him to find a local church to attend in Lincoln so he contacted Roger who invited him to the Quaker meeting.

August went with Roger a few Sundays but the form of service was altogether too solemn and sedate for him. He loved the sense of awe and the peaceful presence of God, but the seemingly endless sitting around in silent meditation didn't appeal to the vibrant new believer at all! He wanted to be praising the Lord in joyful worship all the time.

Roger was aware of August's need for spiritual stimulation and so he said one Sunday morning, "I sometimes go to the service in Newport Hall on a Sunday evening, August. It is quite lively and I think you would enjoy it. Why don't you go along sometime and see what you think."

"Thanks, Roger, I will," August answered enthusiastically. He appreciated his friend's interest and advice, determining to visit Newport Hall that very evening.

And upon doing so he recognised immediately that his search was over.

August had found a sanctuary for his soul!

OVER MY DEAD BODY!

9   The small hall was full. When August was shown to a seat he discovered that the people of all ages sitting around him were singing away with a godly gusto. It seemed as though they meant every word of it.

There was a reality in the sincerity of the worship that August had never come across before. He hadn't been aware that such a place as Lincoln Free Church even existed until Roger had told him about it and he certainly had never imagined that there were people on the planet who could praise God like this!

As he sat there drinking in the atmosphere August felt himself being gently elevated on to a different plane of spiritual experience. This was undoubtedly his level of living, praising the One who had provided him with such profound personal peace.

Although the words of the hymns and choruses that the congregation were singing with such conviction were unfamiliar to him, the theme of them wasn't. This was what impressed August as he sat there in a wonderland of worship.

Every single one of them was about Jesus!

August came close to tears as they sang words that he had never heard before but that expressed so precisely the sentiments of his Saviour-sensitive heart.

'Jesus, Jesus, Jesus,

There is just something about that Name', echoed around repeatedly.

It was sublime, a seventh heaven for August.

If there had been nothing more to the service than the singing, the first-time visitor to this vibrant church would have gone away bountifully blessed.

There was more, though.

When the singing had subsided and an opening prayer had been offered, a man in his late twenties rose to address the congregation. For some reason August had always imagined ministers to be older men, and when a youthful looking Stuart Bell took his place behind the small wooden reading desk he wondered what spiritual sustenance he could offer to the obviously expectant audience.

His misgivings were nothing more than momentary. When the young man had read a portion from the Bible he began to expound it in such a way that August was left mesmerised. The forty-four year old company director was but a babe in Christ, and this young Bible teacher sounded like a mature spiritual giant to him. He spoke with a divine authority and spiritual understanding that completely contradicted his youthful appearance. As Stuart continued to speak, the Book in his hand, most of which had been written more than two millennia before, assumed an amazing relevance for life in Lincoln in the present day.

August sat electrified, hanging on his every word.

He was deeply disappointed when the service came to an end. The time had passed so quickly. He could cheerfully have sat there for another two or three hours, imbibing such inspirational instruction.

Driving home that night on a spiritual high, August determined to attend Lincoln Free Church at every possible opportunity to hear Stuart Bell expound the Scriptures. He had gathered from the announcements made during the service that there was a mid-week Bible teaching meeting when the young pastor was conducting a series of studies on the book of Joshua. How he would look forward to that!

That initial Sunday evening visit to Newport Hall proved to be the beginning of an era of rapid growth in grace for the spiritually ravenous new believer. He never missed a meeting from then on, and spent hours in a personal, in-depth study of the Bible He just couldn't seem to learn enough about his Lord.

It was not long before Stuart became aware of this regular additional member of his audiences. He was delighted to have such an ardent Christian in his meetings for he was an avid listener. August Ericson's eager spiritual intelligence soaked up Biblical truth like blotting paper.

In the early months of 1980 August began to invite Jill to join him in attending the Sunday evening services in Lincoln Free Church. His invitations met with flat refusals at first, Jill's initial reaction being that one religious maniac was enough for any household to maintain. She just couldn't imagine what her commiserating confidantes would say if she went cuckoo as well!

Subconsciously though, and almost in spite of herself, her attitude gradually began to soften. There were probably two reasons for this.

The first was that although August was obsessed with running to every advertised service in his adopted church, and reading his Bible at all hours of the day and night, he remained an extremely devoted husband and father. They all loved him in return, and that was the other reason why his wife began to mellow towards his spiritual musings.

In a strange way she felt sorry for the big, harmless, adorable man that she had loved enough to marry. It came to the stage that she felt everybody was against him, and if that were the case she would be for him. She would stand by her man!

His only abnormality was that he talked non-stop about the Lord, who, he claimed led and guided him in wonderful ways. He might be agreeably divinely eccentric but there was no law against that.

The invitations continued with August focusing on the factor which he knew would sway Jill to join him at church if anything ever did.

"You ought to come with me next Sunday, Jill," he would urge her four or five times every week. "You would really enjoy the music and the singing. It is brilliant!"

Eventually Jill and the family attended a Sunday evening service to please him. Unknown to Jill, this was an answer to many prayers. Although unwilling to admit it at first she was touched by the genuine friendliness of many of the other members of the congregation who made every effort to make her feel at home amongst them. The music appealed to her, too, just as August had so often predicted that it would.

Having begun to attend church regularly with her husband on a Sunday Jill observed how much emphasis the Christian people in the congregation placed on carrying and reading the Bible. This confirmed to her that August was not the only person in Lincoln who had the Bible on the brain. It also gave her an idea.

August was thrilled when Jill presented him with a brand new Bible for his birthday in March. It was one of the most treasured presents that he had ever received. He had been given a copy of his favourite book by his favourite person, who had obviously overcome all her previous prejudices to buy it for him.

Jill was pleased with his undisguised delight at her present, while he considered it not only a lovely gesture but also an answer to prayer.

She may not have been so keen to give her husband a Bible though, if she had been able to foresee what was to happen when he continued reading it.

In an attempt to follow and worship God in a manner that most resembled the teachings of Scripture, August embarked upon a detailed analysis of the practices of the early Christian church. As he studied the opening chapters of the Acts of the Apostles he came upon a procedure in chapter four which caused him to stop long and think hard.

'Neither was there any that lacked', he read, fascinated. 'For as many as were possessors of houses and lands sold them, and brought the prices of the things sold, and laid them down at the apostles' feet: and distribution was made unto every man according as he had need.'

August turned these verses over in his mind for days. He was so anxious to please the Lord in every aspect of his life that he decided to sell all that he had and donate the proceeds to the furtherance of Christian work.

One evening after the midweek meeting he stayed behind to tell the pastor of his conviction.

"Stuart, I have been reading in Acts four and I would like to do as the early disciples and Barnabas did," he began, with the resolution of a man whose mind had already been made up. "I want to sell my house and give you the money to use for the work of Lincoln Free Church."

Stuart was moved by this outright commitment of a life and its means to the Lord, but he also had a very wise head on his young shoulders. He regarded August respectfully for a few moments before venturing any response. It would be important not to be seen to stifle such a heartfelt demonstration of devotion and yet one had to be practical in the circumstances.

"Really, August, the church doesn't need your money," he replied gently, at length. "God has blessed us to such an extent that we are well provided for financially. However, I understand how you feel in your heart and don't want to put you off. Perhaps I could make another suggestion."

"And what's that?" August was keen to know, momentarily afraid that Stuart had considered his proposal either immature or irresponsible.

"If you are convinced that you should sell your house why don't you do that and buy a business and run it for God?" Stuart advised. "You would then be doing something worthwhile with your life while still providing for your family. You could perhaps organise an activity or facility that would see souls brought to the Saviour and Christians strengthened in their faith. Would you be interested in giving that idea some consideration?"

"I most certainly would!" was August's spontaneous reaction. "Thank you, Stuart. You have given me a lot to think about!"

As he considered the concept on the way home August became increasingly excited about it. That was it! Sell up, buy a business and run it for God. Why had he never thought of that before?

By the time he arrived in his own drive August was completely consumed with the idea. He was so prepossessed that it hadn't dawned on him that other people might view his proposal from a different perspective!

"Jill, I'm going to sell the house, love!" he burst out as soon as he and his wife were alone in the living room. "Then I will use the money to buy a business and run it for God!"

"If you sell this house, August, it will be over my dead body!" Jill retorted, immediately and angrily. "I have been trying to go along with you in your divine dreams and heavenly hallucinations, but this is a step too far! There is no way that you are selling this house over our heads!"

Having fired her final salvo she left the room, closing the door firmly behind her.

August was left alone with his thoughts.

His wife had just stuck a pin in his shiny new balloon.

What was he going to do now?

THE SIGN OF THE FISH

10

August was thrown into a quandary.

Jill's objections, rather than putting him off, seemed to leave him even more determined to put his house on the market and, using the administrative skills acquired over the years, buy a business to manage for God. There were rare moments of weakness, though, when he began to consider the practicalities of such a project and wonder how it could be achieved.

It was an honourable aspiration, but was it feasible?

Or could it be, as Jill would be apt to suggest, just another of his illogical, celestial fantasies?

It couldn't be, for it wouldn't go away.

Although he had been extremely happy for many years in Mawer and Collingham's, August began to feel inexplicably restless in the job he loved. It was as though he sensed that he wasn't going to belong in that respected store for very much longer. There was something else up ahead for him. But what?

If he was to sell the house, even over Jill's dead body, and buy a business, what should it be? Where could he be most effective for God?

The answer came to him in almost the same way as his conversion conviction. He woke up at three o'clock one morning with the pressing problem of his life uppermost in his mind. This was no session of rambling, drowsy dreams. August was wide-awake.

Two phrases which he had heard used in Christian contexts seemed to have fixed themselves firmly in his head. They rotated, as though jockeying for position, each clamouring to claim his absolute attention.

They were 'The Upper Room' and 'The Sign of the Fish'.

He felt he could dispense with the idea of The Sign of the Fish straight away. The name suggested something to August which he did not find at all appealing. It was a fish restaurant, and as he had no experience whatsoever in the frying of fish he dismissed it out of hand.

The Upper Room idea was different.

August began to mull this over in his mind and as he did he thought of an upstairs room above the Co-op grocery store right beside the church. He began to consider the possibility of starting a drop-in centre there, serving tea or coffee and a scone and selling attractive Christian literature and tapes. In that way people could have a place to meet their friends for a chat, and yet the staff, who would be carefully selected Christians, could use it as a bridge to make a diplomatic presentation of the Gospel.

It was exciting. He could just imagine it. The smell of freshly brewed coffee, cloth-covered tables each with a posy of flowers, and a stand beside the till offering well presented free Gospel literature. There would also be books, Bibles and tapes for sale and soft Christian music playing though a PA system...

That must surely be it. August barely slept for the remainder of the night for he was so busy organising the Upper Room!

Days passed. Then they ran into weeks.

August still dreamt of the Upper Room, but when he made enquiries about procuring the room, which he had mentally earmarked for its establishment, he was frustrated to find that there were difficulties. It seemed that his initial vision was not to become a reality after all. Was this a sign that perhaps he should remain in his present position and serve the Lord whom he loved from there?

No. August didn't think so. There must be something else, something different out there. Although he had only been a Christian for six months he had heard speakers say more than once that 'when God closes one door He always opens another one.'

The room above the Co-op wasn't the only upstairs room to let in Lincoln. God would work His purpose out for August's life, sooner or later. In the meantime he would continue to lean upon the Lord and pray constantly and earnestly for His guidance.

Remaining convinced that he would be starting a business, somewhere, sometime, for God, he took the bold step of tendering his resignation to shocked colleagues in Mawer and Collingham's in April. July 31st would be his last day in the store. From then on he would be out on his own, with God.

Before giving notice in the store he told his wife what he was planning to do and she was horrified. "Don't worry, love," August tried to console her. I have committed my life to the Lord. He will look after us."

"The Lord…The Lord…The Lord…Here we go again," Jill repeated softly. "Always the Lord. I just hope you're right, August!"

It was noticeable that Jill was now more willing to express a weary resignation to her husband's spiritual pronouncements than she had ever been before. She had by then been attending Lincoln Free Church for a couple of months and recognised the complete sincerity of most of the members whom she had met from that fellowship. And although she wasn't aware of it, almost the entire congregation had joined August in fervent personal prayer for her salvation.

Her continued attendance at the church which was up the hill in the north end of the city allowed August and she to become friendly with the pastor, Stuart, and he soon became a regular and welcome visitor to the Ericson home. Every time he called Stuart prayed with the family and Jill soon found herself, despite herself, listening with interest to what he had to say. The pastor was able to explain issues like sin and salvation, or life and death to her without her feeling in any way pressurised.

It seemed to make sense when Stuart said it.

These visits, combined with the weekly sermons at the church services, led Jill to realise that she needed Christ in her life every bit as much as August had done.

When all the barriers of resistance she had erected to shield herself from the barrage of religious hysteria that had entered her home crumbled before her, she yearned to be saved. One evening, when she could endure.the spiritual tug-of-war that had begun within her soul no longer, Jill phoned Stuart and asked him to come round and speak to her.

The pastor, who had been praying that he would receive such a call for months, was happy to oblige and on July 18, 1980, he led her to simple faith in Christ.

Family circumstances changed dramatically from that moment.

The house could only have been put up for sale 'over Jill's dead body'.

Now, though, the dead body had been removed!

Paul described the process that had taken place when writing to some Christians in Ephesus, back in Bible times.

'As for you,' he taught them, 'you who were dead in your transgressions and sins, in which you used to live when you followed the ways of this world…. God, who is rich in mercy, made us alive with Christ even when we were dead in transgression. It is by grace you have been saved…'

Jill was now alive in Christ, and shared the same new nature that she had found so difficult to appreciate in her husband for the previous ten months.

A spiritual spin-off to this united family front in Christ was that August could put the house up for sale.

Over Jill's living body!

As soon as he had contacted estate agents to put his home on the market, August began searching the classified columns of the newspapers and the local property vendors in the hunt for a business to buy.

The only establishment for sale in the city at that time within his estimated price bracket was a small fish and chip shop and café in a dilapidated area of the city beside the market. The buildings in Sincil Street, where the café was located had been earmarked for demolition and redevelopment, and hence the whole street was in need of repair. The street had been saved from an assault by the bulldozers only because of its historical significance, as many of the buildings were over four hundred years old.

On making enquiries August was intrigued to discover that the reserve price he had placed on the house exactly matched the asking price for the business.

Convinced that he should follow this single lead further, August walked across the city centre from his spacious, air-conditioned office in Mawer and Collingham's to this run-down, greasy, side-street café. He climbed the narrow stairs and took a seat at a small table covered with tea-stained cigarette-scarred oilcloth. This was a world away from the linen tablecloths and hygienic cleanliness of the in-store restaurant where he would normally have relaxed over lunch.

The prospective buyer ordered the standard fare from the slimy menu, fish, chips and mushy peas and then sat surveying the smoky squalor of the place, while he waited for it to be served. When his 'meal' was presented to him after five or ten minutes August discovered that more than the peas could have been classified as 'mushy'. The whole plate was a soggy, mushy mess.

August bowed his head and really appreciated, for the first time in his life, why Christians insisted in praying over their food!

Although there had never been a paintbrush on the grubby walls of that café for years, and the entire property had been allowed to lapse into a very neglected state, August was encouraged by the steady stream of customers coming and going around him. If we bought this place and did a massive clean up job on it, I believe we could make a go of it for God, he kept trying to convince himself over and over again over his unappealing plate.

When he had finished he went downstairs to pay and asked to speak to Mrs. Hunt, the owner. After some discussion he agreed a price with her and returned to his plush office in Mawer and Collingham's, the prospective proprietor of a run-down fish and chip shop.

Going home that evening would be the biggest hurdle he would ever have to surmount on the road to fulfilling his God-given vision, he reckoned. How was he going to tell Jill what he had just done?

He prayed that God would help her to see the potential of that decrepit little café for Him. Then he spent most of the afternoon preparing his case, argument by argument, for the big presentation.

If they worked hard and cleaned it up they could turn it around. There would be lots of people willing to help, no doubt. They could advertise it in the local press. They could ask the church to pray, and so it went on.

When it came to the moment of truth, however, and he arrived home to inform Jill of the transaction he had agreed, she took it all remarkably calmly. This was another proof to August, not that he needed one, that God answers prayer.

"It will be a challenge, darling," was her measured response. "But I know we can do it. God will help us, and so, I'm sure, will some of the people from the church."

Then she paused, as though almost embarrassed by her own enthusiasm, "But we still haven't sold the house yet," she cautioned. "So where are we going to find the money to pay for it?"

"I believe the Lord has a buyer for the house, too, Jill," August assured her, trying to sound more confident that he felt at that particular moment. "We just have to keep on praying."

Jill smiled, but said nothing. She just thought, 'There he goes on the Lord again.'

This time, though, she believed him.

The Lord had done so much for them both already. And He hadn't finished with them yet either.

Their earnest prayers were answered within days.

Miracles began to take place in rapid succession before their eyes.

Their house was sold to a buyer with the funds available, and who was desperate to move in. Spacious rented accommodation was procured in an area convenient to schools and their new project premises.

Late summer that year became a time of frenetic activity. August had to say goodbye to his many friends in Mawer and Collingham's, and then he and Jill hurried to move house before the schools recommenced.

When all this was done they began to look forward to signing up for their new property and taking possession of it on 1st September.

It was hard not to let the waiting become frustrating. The pair planned and prayed and discussed but all they had of their new business to date was its name.

When August told Jill of the previously discarded option from his middle of the night in the middle of March revelation they agreed that God had given them the name, long before he had shown them the chip-shop-cum-café.

It had to be Sign Of The Fish.

LICENSED TO KILL

11 It was with anticipation tinged with a slight trepidation that August and Jill made their way down to Sincil Street that Monday morning. September 1st had come at last and the property that they had prayed so much about had become theirs.

Their first act was to dedicate their new acquisition and the enterprise upon which they were about to embark, to the Lord. They were acutely aware, however, that the local health inspector would not approve of the selection of their Heavenly Father's furry, flying and creeping creations that had taken up residence there. In an attempt to redress that situation the first person to follow them over the door that morning was the man from Rentokil.

Dressed in an overall, and with hands and arms bedecked with an array of buckets and packets, sprayers and puffers, he introduced himself. "Good morning, my name is Bond," he announced. "I am licensed to kill."

August smiled silently to himself.

'When my Lord sends somebody to do a job for one of His children, He always sends the best,' he mused. 'Surely 007 will soon sort this little lot out!'

Resisting the temptation to make a joke about the relationship between man's name and his profession, August gave him the go ahead to proceed with the job he had come to do, but with one significant stipulation.

"You have my permission to kill every living thing within the walls of this building," he authorised, "but spare Jill and me. We are hoping to run a business here when you are finished!"

Mr. Rentokil Bond made an initial inspection of the property, accompanied by a lot of shaking of the head in disbelief, then set to work.

There was no time to waste. He had a full two days work ahead of him.

The shop had lain empty for a month while all the legalities were being seen to, and in that time a motley collection of creatures had decided to squat there to await either eviction or execution.

Families of mice scuttled for shelter and armies of cockroaches crunched below everyone's feet. Discarded containers had become the breeding ground for enough maggots to keep all the fishermen in Lincoln supplied with bait for the remainder of their angling lives. The bluebottles that had become too bloated to continue buzzing about were crawling up down and all around over everything, everywhere, from the floor to the ceiling. Slugs of prehistoric proportions slithered slimily over the sinks in the potato preparation room out at the back.

To eradicate that assortment of undesirables was a mammoth task, but when it was complete another equally daunting challenge lay up ahead. How were they ever going to have this place cleaned up sufficiently to meet the standards of both the Environmental Health Officer and Jill, whose days in nursing had made her super sensitive to the importance of food hygiene?

The only answer appeared to be to enlist help.

August and Jill contacted a number of Christians whom they had known to be unemployed, and their friend and pastor, Stuart

Bell. This clean-up brigade worked tirelessly for weeks, using bottles of detergent by the dozen. They did a total, ruthless throw-out and scrub-down job. All the burnt black, greased coated kitchen equipment except the fish fryer was transported to the local dump. Then the ceiling, walls and floor were thoroughly scoured. New tables and chairs were purchased for the former furniture had also to be discarded.

Slowly, gradually, the shop began to look like an establishment where food could be safely served.

The big test for the new café owners and their band of volunteers would come when the Environmental Health officer came to call. Would their efforts pass the close scrutiny of an expert eye?

They needn't have feared. Having had long-running problems at that particular address for years he was delighted to see it in its sanitised state. He was so pleased that he swung Jill around in a dance of celebration in the back yard.

While the purging of the premises was taking place the impact of another important consideration began to dawn on August and Jill. How did you open a fish and chip shop when you had never fried fish and chips in big quantities before? The thought of boiling fat sent a freezing chill down August's spine.

This time the only solution seemed to be to seek help from those who knew.

Mr. Hagan at Mr. Chips of Louth and David Tate of Tate's of Boston both gave August and Jill lessons in commercial fish frying on slacker evenings in their shops. Although he still firmly believed that God wanted them to open a fish and chip shop and café and run it for Him, August was beginning to have his reservations. The prospect of standing over a vat of boiling fat, day after day, filled him more with dread than delight he had to confess.

Having gutted the place to have it fumigated and decontaminated God's trainee fish fryers were faced with the challenge of redecorating and reequipping it to the high standards, not only sanitary but spiritual, that they had set for themselves. It was their aim that everyone who entered their café should be very conscious of its Christian ethos.

A sign-writer was employed to change the name at the front of the shop. Puzzled passers by, and indeed some nearby traders watched with interest as the words SIGN OF THE FISH were painted in bold brown letters on the cream board above the window.

What on earth could that mean?

That was exactly the kind of question the owners had hoped their customers would be compelled to ask. It would afford them an immediate opportunity to speak of the formation of the early Christian church, and then tell of the need for faith in Christ.

The words of John chapter three and verse sixteen, 'For God so loved the world, that He gave his only begotten Son that whosoever believeth in Him, should not perish but should have everlasting life,' were painted on both sides of the door between the carry-out counter and the sit-down café. The freshly painted walls were adorned with attractive Scripture text posters and toast-racks containing tracts were placed on all the shiny new tables. A sound system played Gospel music softly in the background, and a number of the unemployed Christians who had helped in the clean-up operation volunteered to stay on as preparation staff and waitresses. These men and women, though enthusiastic, were as equally unskilled as August and Jill, and therefore just as fearful of the prospect of opening day as their employers.

When all the necessary preparations were almost complete Wednesday 22nd October 1980, was set as opening day. Since August and Jill had relied on the guidance of God in prayer throughout every step and stage of the buying of the business and the refurbishment of the premises, they determined that every day in the Sign Of The Fish would begin with prayer. God was going to have His place in their business, where they felt He should be. That was first. If anyone came who could play a guitar and lead them in singing, then they would sing His praise. Otherwise they would hear His Word, and then commit each day, with all its opportunities and possible problems, to Him.

When that long awaited Wednesday morning finally arrived a somewhat nervous staff met to pray before opening for business. August beseeched the Lord audibly for abundant blessing on the business, as they sought to run it in His name and for His glory. Silently, though, his sensible self was saying, 'But don't go too heavy on the blessing for a day or two, Lord. At least not until I have mastered the fish-frying!'

A steady stream, but not a rushing mighty river, of curious, but seemingly satisfied people passed through 'the fish and chip shop with the funny name', on that opening day. The more observant of them were amused to see the new boss working away in white apron and hat, with L-plates strung on either end of the frying range.

The takings that Wednesday amounted to seventy-two pounds. August and Jill felt that this initial income from The Sign Of The Fish belonged to the One who had never needed an L-plate for anything. That was Jesus, who had no problem in supplying His disciples with fried fish for breakfast after a singularly unsuccessful night's fishing on the Sea of Galilee.

August saved that seventy-two pounds until the following Sunday. Then he divided it out amongst the family and between them they placed the entire takings of their first day's trading in the offering baskets at Lincoln Free Church.

It was their presentation of first fruits unto the Lord.

I'LL GIVE YOU A TIP

12

The shop became increasingly busy.

News spread quickly amongst the chip-consuming community around Lincoln city centre that there was a new café in Sincil Street. It had a funny name, but the fish and chips were really delicious. They did a lovely line in mushy peas as well.

Many of those who were attracted to the Sign Of The Fish by the advertising campaign, or had it recommended to them by others, soon became regular customers.

These diners, very appreciative of the high standard of friendly service they had come to enjoy began leaving tips for the staff on the tables. This presented the waitresses with a problem, for if they accepted the tips it would mean that they would have to pay Income Tax on their earnings. It was a peculiar predicament to be in, because the spontaneous generosity of grateful customers was creating a crisis of conscience for the ultra-honest Christian staff.

The issue was raised one morning at prayer time and the staff, led by August and Jill, brought the matter to the Lord in prayer. This had become their established pattern when important decisions had to be made in the business.

"Lord, what do we do with these tips?" was the burden of the corporate requests that morning. "This is money which we are being kindly given but don't need. We feel that it could be used somehow in the promotion of your Kingdom."

When intercession time was over and resolution time arrived, various possible solutions were aired. With everyone making very practical suggestions one girl popped up with an idea that seemed to capture the imagination of all.

"In our church recently they were talking about sponsoring underprivileged children. I was wondering if perhaps we could undertake to support a child in the Third World?" she proposed.

It was unanimously and enthusiastically decided that this was an extremely satisfactory way in which to sort out their dilemma. They would sponsor a needy child with the tips received, and if the income from this source proved insufficient to meet that need then the business would make up any shortfall.

August made enquiries about agencies that operated sponsorship programmes and discovered that both Tear Fund and Bible Lands had suitable schemes. It was decided that Sign of The Fish would endeavour to support one named child from each of these organisations.

The next challenge was to tell the tipping patrons of their decision.

A solution to this situation came one day when August and Jill were on a day out to Sheffield. They had called into a restaurant for a meal, and being by then restaurateurs themselves they were always on the lookout for new ideas.

"Look at that, Jill," August enthused, sounding as though he had just discovered the Niagara Falls. "The menu is the place mat. That's brilliant! We could make use of that idea back in Sign Of The Fish. It would save us a lot of time running around with menus at busy periods and we could provide information for our clients on it too. Like about the sponsorship scheme for instance."

Back home in Lincoln next day August set about designing a placemat menu, and in addition to the prices of everything from fish and chips and mushy peas to sausages and curry sauce, it contained two other items of information.

The first of these was to draw the attention of customers to the tracts on the racks on the tables, inviting anyone interested to take one home to read, 'free of charge'.

Down in the bottom right hand corner he made clear the position in relation to the tips. Eye-catching photographs of the children they were sponsoring had been mounted on the walls of the first floor dining room, where most of the tables were. The announcement attracted attention to them indirectly by stating simply, 'For your information, all tips received on these premises go to help support a child in the Third World.'

It was amazing what began to happen after that!

The total in tips started to increase dramatically. This resulted in August, Jill and the staff having to keep considering sponsoring more and more children!

After a few moths August realized that the early days of the week were slacker in Sign Of The Fish. As the reputation of the restaurant grew, Friday and Saturday became very busy days with queues often forming in the street outside the shop. This didn't happen from Monday to Thursday. There were always a number of customers in and out but August felt that there could be more.

Who, though, were they? Or even, where were they?

Could they, perhaps, be old age pensioners with plenty of time, but not a lot of money, to spend?

When considering how to attract some of the city's senior citizens to Sign Of The Fish, August remembered the philosophy of a friend of his who ran a bus company. He often said that he would rather have a bus full of passengers paying 'two bob' a time as have three people on it at a two pound fare.

Since their aim was not to make a whopping profit, but to expose people to the Gospel by various means, August and Jill introduced a cut-price menu for pensioners. They advertised on the menu, and also in the local press, that all meals would be half-price for old age pensioners from Monday-Thursday inclusive.

This worked well for at least two reasons, one obvious, and the other less so.

Initially the local pensioners were drawn by the prospect of a high-quality but half-price meal. There was, however, an unexpected but nonetheless welcome social spin off to this initiative. It was a stark fact which August and Jill had never considered in the midst of the hustle and bustle of their busy lives. Many of those who were to later become their elderly regulars were unbelievably lonely! They came, not only for the meal, but also to simply sit for an hour in the same room as a few other human beings.

Since some of their larger tables had places for six people, Jill, who kept a watching eye on all that happened 'out on the floor', became adept at seating them together.

Seeing an elderly lady sitting alone and looking rather lost, having placed her order and waiting for her meal to arrive, for example, Jill would arrive silently by her side.

"Excuse me, my darling, and what's your name?" she would enquire in her open, affable manner.

"Oh, I'm Mrs. Roberts," might come the rather startled reply.

"Yes, O.K. love, that's nice. But what's your Christian name?" Jill would persist.

"It's Agnes, why?" the puzzled customer might volunteer sheepishly.

"Well this is Edna, " Jill would go on, gesturing to the woman who had been hovering at the top of the stairs, unable to find a seat. She seemed to be about the same age as the awestruck Agnes. "Do you mind if she joins you today? We are a bit short of seats at the minute."

"No, not at all," Agnes would say, inwardly glad that she was going to have someone sitting with her, actually at the table.

The two ladies would begin to chat and it often happened that Jill would have the joy of seeing people like Edna and Agnes, whom she had introduced, sitting having a meal together two weeks later. With some couples this became a regular weekly rendezvous, having become friends and arranged to meet.

That was very rewarding.

With the sponsorship of needy children in far-off lands and concession meals for struggling pensioners in his home city both well established, August was having his own personal time of Scripture reading and prayer one morning before breakfast at home.

He had just begun to read in the Epistle of James that day and discovered an interesting phrase in the last verse of the first chapter. Before even referring to the notes he had bought to help him in his study he read the verse over again a couple of times.

'Pure religion and undefiled before God and the Father is this, To visit the fatherless and widows in their affliction, and to keep himself unspotted from the world', it said.

The words 'the fatherless and widows in their affliction' seemed to jump off the page at him. These were the two kinds of people who had been benefiting most to date from their efforts at the Sign of the Fish chip shop, orphans and widows. Donations were being sent to relieve the affliction of at least a few from one of the groups overseas, and the shop in Sincil Street was continuing to prove a sanctuary for the other category in Lincoln.

"Thank You, Lord. Thank You for revealing that to me," August breathed in prayerful worship as he sank to his knees. "We are obeying Your command in our work at Sign Of The Fish."

13 THERE'S SOMETHING YOU OUGHT TO KNOW

It seemed that everything was on the up-and-up. The widows and orphans were being well catered for through Sign Of The Fish. The amount of money raised by the use of the table tips to sponsor impoverished children in the Third World continued to increase and the half-price menu had seen a regular Monday-Thursday customer base established. Many of these elderly people had come to look upon their weekly outings to the fish restaurant, and the opportunity it afforded for a leisurely chat with some newly found friends, as highlights of an otherwise humdrum existence.

This had been gratifying at first.

People seemed quite at ease coming continually into the Sign Of The Fish chip shop. It had become a popular meeting point, with its soft Christian music and overt presentation of the Christian message in both text and tract all over the place.

It was almost a year after opening before August began to feel uneasy with the way things were going. He started to ask himself if this was why he and Jill had undertaken this project with all the guidance from God they had enjoyed and all the hassles they had endured. Surely both he and God had intended it to be more than just a sort of an upmarket charitable community care centre serving fish and chips instead of the standard tea and biscuits.

August's vision had been to see people brought to know Jesus Christ as Saviour through the influence of Sign Of The Fish.

There was no question but that the texts were being read, for nobody but their few blind patrons could miss them. They were in big bold letters on every suitable spot. Nor could there be any doubt about the tracts. Hundreds of them must have been taken, for they were constantly being replaced.

In his more philosophical theological moments August reminded himself of seed in the soil. It takes time to progress from seed to shoot to plant to flower to fruit. Jesus had shown in His teachings that He understood all the processes involved in, and the inherent unpredictability of, seed germination and fruit production. Paul, too, had hinted that spiritual harvests needed time to mature when he wrote about one preacher planting and another one watering, with God Himself providing the eventual increase.

That was all fine in theory, but they had been praying away and frying away for nearly twelve months and not even a single shoot of salvation had seemed to appear above the ground.

In his more fervent, and more frustrated, moments, August expected miracles.

Surely the God who had revealed Himself to a whole array of needy characters, some of them in most unsavoury situations, could lead someone to trust in Him through Sign Of The Fish.

It hadn't happened.

Not one single person had read a tract at a table and abandoned their chips and mushy peas to throw themselves down on their knees and cry out in anguish, 'What must I do to be saved?'

What was wrong?

August shared his concerns with Jill at home and with the other members of staff in the morning prayer sessions. They decided to pray all the more earnestly that God would lead someone to faith in Christ through the witness of the restaurant.

After a few more months of waiting their prayers were answered when a lady came to the door of Sign Of The Fish, with her son who was in a wheelchair.

The main dining room was upstairs and inaccessible to the disabled, but there was a limited space where wheelchairs could be accommodated on the ground floor. Some of the staff were only two willing to help the prospective new customer find a place at a table and make room for her son, whom she introduced as John.

When settled, the lady studied the menu for a few moments before giving her order to one of the waitresses. As the meal was placed before her the visitor remarked to the girl who had served her, "You know for some reason I felt strangely compelled to come here. I heard about your chip shop from somebody who had been, and I came along for I felt that you might know how to help me. I have had a lot of problems down the years and long to experience some measure of lasting peace in my life."

Realising that this particular client had a hunger in her heart that could not be satisfied by fish and chips, the staff member removed her apron and became transformed from waitress to counsellor in a matter of seconds. Janet Muxlow, the woman with the craving in her heart, poured out the sad story of an empty, unfulfilled life into the sympathetic ear of the listener. When she was sure that Janet had finished the woman in whom she had confided took the opportunity to reassure her that there was a solution to all problems.

She sat and explained to the disillusioned lady how that Jesus Christ had come to earth to die on a cross to provide forgiveness of sin and peace with God to all who believed in Him.

Janet sat mesmerised. She confessed to never having heard such a message of hope and love before. Yes, she said, she had always been aware that Jesus had died on a cross about Easter time, but she had never realised that His death had anything to do with her.

As the pair sat chatting, with John looking on, the other staff were praying as they went about their duties. Could this be the ordinary working day in which God was going to answer their heartfelt prayers in an extraordinary way?

It was.

Before she left to take John home, well over an hour after arriving at the door of Sign Of The Fish, Janet had opened her heart to the Lord Jesus.

There was a great sense of rejoicing amongst the staff that evening and next morning at praying and sharing time. God had sealed all the work and witness in that little fish and chip restaurant with the blessing of salvation.

The thrill that August experienced was tinged by an inescapable sense of contrition on his part. Why was I so doubtful? Or was it just that I was too impatient? he wondered.

He felt particularly chastened when he remembered the words of the first verse of Psalm 40, as he drove into work the next day.

'I waited patiently for the Lord; and he inclined unto me and heard my cry,' he repeated over to himself a time or two, with a wry smile. The Lord had inclined unto him and heard his cry. It was the waiting patiently bit that he had found difficult after the first six months or so!

Having experienced the blessing of the Lord in marvellous ways up until that point he ought to have known He wouldn't fail him on Sign Of The Fish.

August had learnt two lessons for the price of one experience. He had discovered that God is faithful in answering our prayers, but that He will provide the response in His time, not at our whim.

Janet's conversion seemed to be the icing on the cake of blessing for Sign Of The Fish. And it led August to contemplate expansion.

It was obvious that the café in Sincil Street could be considered a success, whatever way you looked at it. People who had heard of it had travelled quite considerable distances to pay it a visit. Queues formed outside the shop and along the street every Saturday. Contributions towards the sponsorship of their 'adopted children' had continued to grow and they had been able to forward occasional financial donations towards the furtherance of Christian work both at home and overseas.

Surely it would be a good idea if we were to enlarge our scope by putting a number of mobile fish and chip vans on the road, he reasoned. This would enable us to make even more money for the Lord's work as well as bringing the Gospel message to the outlying villages.

The more he thought of it, the more feasible, possibly even sensible, it seemed to become in his mind. Saturday had always been a hectic day in the shop and August had begun many Saturdays by arriving down to work at four o'clock in the morning. There he pre-fried up to forty bowls of chips. With these available the waiting time for customers at busy periods was greatly reduced. This pre-fried chip was far superior to the frozen chip, in his estimation.

As August pursued his solitary early morning early frying routine one Saturday he had another bright idea. What if he were to produce enough pre-fried chips to supply not only the fish and chip Gospel mobiles he was planning, but also some of the small caterers in the city and the surrounding areas as well?

That could be a moneymaking enterprise.

Firmly convinced that he could expand his business into something that would benefit both God and himself, August took over a small industrial unit on the outskirts of Lincoln. He purchased three fish and chip mobiles, fitted them out with new pan fryers and put them on the road. His pre-fried pre-packed chips were also to be distributed from his industrial unit.

Big business here I come, thought August Ericson.

The only problem was that August had embarked upon a project that he thought would be beneficial to the work of God, without ever talking to God about it. He had become so expert in preparing chips and frying fish that he thought he could manage everything on his own.

That was not how it worked out, however.

Within months the cost of keeping the mobiles on the road became prohibitive, adding to his already formidable burden of debt. The business began to experience serious difficulties with cash flow.

August was on the verge of bankruptcy.

The family home had to be sold to pay off mounting debts.

All his business assets had to go, except Sign Of The Fish.

August, Jill and the growing family were forced to return to living in rented accommodation.

Another lesson, and this time an extremely bitter one, had been learnt.

During a fearful and tearful repentance August recognised that he had overstepped himself, having tried to race on ahead of God. His Heavenly Father had given him a clear vision of the Sign Of The Fish, and that was all. If He was going to accomplish anything in His servant's life it would be there, and there alone. To comply with God's will for him, August would have to bury his dreams of big business and settle himself in that inauspicious little shop in Sincil Street.

He had no choice in the matter really.

It was all he had left.

Waiting for Janet's conversion had caused him some intense spiritual soul-searching. The outcome, though, had been delightful.

Coping with the distinct possibility of self-inflicted bankruptcy had caused him untold sleepless nights, and his family considerable physical inconvenience.

The end result of that situation had been devastating.

By the time everything was set to rights August had come to consider himself a Special Needs pupil in the School of God.

It had taken him a long time to come to terms with the divine declaration of Isaiah chapter nine.

'My thoughts are not your thoughts, neither are your ways my ways, saith the Lord.

For as the heavens are higher than the earth, so are my ways higher than your ways, and my thoughts than your thoughts.'

Those had been hard lessons to learn.

JUST GIVE HIM A HAND, LORD

14 Strange things often happened to August in August. And August 1984 was no exception.

The Ericson family had some friends from America staying with them that month in the house which a Christian businessman had let to them in an exclusive part of Lincoln.

It was a Thursday afternoon and August had begun to think of finishing frying for the day. There were a few members of the serving staff and some lingering customers who, having paid their money were determined to make the most of their last minutes, in Sign Of The Fish. One or two outstanding orders stood waiting to be completed.

August looked up at the clock. They would be closing in half-an-hour. Soon he would be with the others. It was a lovely sunny summer afternoon. Perhaps they would all be eating outside together later that evening.

He was frying in one pan and as he did so glanced instinctively across at the other one. Suddenly he was shocked out of his subconscious automated state. The lid of the pan was closed but puffs of smoke were squirting out from below it all the way round.

August realised, to his horror, that he hadn't switched the pan off, and as it was not thermostatically controlled, it had overheated.

Reaching across, he opened the lid of the pan.

A cloud of blue smoke shot up to the ceiling. The pan was about to catch fire.

In an impulsive attempt to reduce the temperature the frightened fish-fryer picked up a bowl of prepared chips and tossed them into the pan of smoking fat. Unfortunately, in his haste August didn't notice that the water in which the chips were steeping hadn't been drained off

There was an explosion and an eruption of flame when the cold water hit the boiling fat.

August's right had was completely engulfed by fat on fire.

He shrieked in agony.

Rushing to the cold-water tap he held his hand below it then plunged it into a bowl of cold water that Jill had run for him. Someone dialled 999 and within a short space of time an ambulance had drawn up at the door.

The paramedics wrapped the burnt hand up tightly and whisked August off to Hospital. So much for the leisurely period of relaxation on a balmy summer's evening!

The charge nurse at casualty and then a doctor examined August's scorched hand. Skin had been burnt off it in a number of places. Every time they touched it to make their examination he squirmed in anguish. The pain was excruciating.

Although he was in absolute agony August had only one question for the medical staff.

"How long will it be before this hand heals?" was his sole concern. He was thinking of his responsibilities at Sign Of The Fish. How could a right-handed fish fryer fry fish without a right hand? Jill and some other members of staff had been trained on the pans and could carry on the business in the short term, but certainly not forever.

The doctor kept glancing down at the seared hand as he predicted, "It will probably be at least six months before you will be able to do anything with it. And even then the hand may not return to full function."

Six months! Even then possibly not full function.

What were they going to do without him in Sign Of The Fish for six months?!

And what if his hand never retuned to normal?

It didn't bear thinking about.

When business was finished for the day Jill drove up to the Hospital to collect her husband in the car. As they were leaving, with August's hand enveloped in a 'Falklands dressing', and his pockets stuffed with painkillers, the nurse said, "You will have to return here every day for quite a while, Mr. Ericson, to have the dressing changed. We will see you tomorrow."

You will have to return to the hospital every day. You just MIGHT have the use of your hand in six months. Announcements like these, made in such a matter-of fact manner, tormented August's mind that night. They, though, came in a very poor second on the table of torture to the virtually unbearable throbbing pain in his bandaged hand.

Dick Heaney, the pastor from Pennsylvania who was staying with the Ericson family, had hired a car for the duration of his holiday in Britain. Feeling sorry no doubt for the host with the hurting hand he invited August to join him and his two sons, Gary and Tom, on a trip they had planned the next day.

That Friday morning Dick arrived down to breakfast with his big idea. "Gee, August," he remarked, "You will hardly be going into work today. We are hoping to go to York for the day. We will take you to the Hospital to have your dressing changed, and then you could come with us. O.K?"

August knew that he would have to stay away from Sincil Street for some time and his sense of frustration was fuelled by the prospect of a period of enforced inactivity. Yet his pain was so constant that he was unable to concentrate on anything for more than five or ten minutes. It was very kind of Dick and the boys to invite him, and it would pass some of the long day stretching out ahead, but August wasn't sure whether he wanted to go or not. He felt that if he had to be miserable it would be better to be miserable in the relative comfort of home than out on a sightseeing spin somewhere.

Having asked for half an hour to make up his mind August eventually consented to accompany his friends on their day out. He loved York and anyway it would seem very rude to refuse their guest's kind offer. They were obviously only trying to be helpful.

As they sped northwards in the car August was in agony. The two young lads chattered excitedly all the way and he felt obliged to act as the knowledgeable English tourist guide and respond to all their questions and comments. This proved difficult to do without revealing the wretchedness, both mental and physical, which he felt.

On reaching their destination August asked to be excused the tramp around the tourist trail in the city of York. He pointed his guests in the general direction of the famous Minster and then sat down on a summer seat for a session of solitary suffering and self-pity.

After half-an-hour he decided that he would attempt to deaden the pain in his hand by downing a couple more of the painkilling tablets on which he had come to depend so much in the previous twenty-four hours. It was then that he came across a problem which he hadn't envisaged. Normally he would have been taking these at home, with Jill or some of the children to help, but how now did he manage to unscrew the lid off the bottle with the use of only one hand?

He struggled with it but to no avail. No matter how hard he tried to prop the bottle up for stability, as soon as he began to unscrew the lid with his unfamiliar left hand, the bottle turned round with him.

It was exasperating.

A little old lady, who had been sitting on a seat almost directly opposite the beleaguered burns victim with the impressive looking Falklands dressing on his right hand, spotted his dilemma.

Taking pity on him she rose from her seat and toddled across.

"Can I help you, son?" she enquired softly in a voice laden with compassion but crackling with age.

"Yes. Perhaps you could take the lid off that bottle for me," August replied gratefully.

August's volunteer aide was perhaps thirty years older than he was, but she had the decided advantage of the use of both hands. With what seemed minimal effort she opened the bottle and placed two welcome painkillers in his outstretched left hand. These were then transferred to the mouth in succession and swallowed with successive gulps.

Satisfied that her mission of mercy had been adequately executed the charming elderly lady left with the heartfelt thanks of the struggling sufferer on the seat ringing in her ears.

When Dick and the boys returned to where they had left their guide for the day they all began the short walk back to where they had parked the car. Gary and Tom were treating August to an enthusiastic summary of where they had been and what they had seen when their dad interrupted them.

"Hold on a minute there, boys," he begged. "I want to ask August something."

When granted the favour of half-a-minute's silence he proceeded with his question.

"How far is the Hollybush Farm Christian Fellowship from here, August?" he wanted to know. "I have heard about it from a number of folk. They have a meeting there tonight I think. Perhaps we could give it a call if it isn't too far away."

August camouflaged an inward sigh with an outward smile.

The last thing he wanted to do at that time of the evening was head off to Hollybush Farm but if it would make Dick's day he could do it.

"Considering the distances you are used to driving back home you probably wouldn't think it very far. It is at Northallerton which is at the very most an hour from here," he informed the interested pastor. He hoped secretly than an extra hour's drive towards the end of the day *would* prove too far, but was not surprised to be disappointed.

"Oh that's nothing," Dick's response was immediate. "Do you mind if we go on up there, August, seeing we are so close?"

"No, I don't mind at all, " August replied. This was not strictly true, but helpful hosts are noted for going to any length to facilitate their guests, whatever the cost either in effort or honesty.

When they arrived at the Hollybush Farm Fellowship that evening August introduced Dick and his sons to some of the elders there, whom he knew. With the presentations complete he guided his friends into a seat near the back of the auditorium. All August wanted to do was allow them to savour the Hollybush Farm Christian Fellowship experience, then set off for home as soon as possible.

Whether some of his elders informed him, or whether he had just noticed his friend in the audience August couldn't be quite sure, but when Pastor Jim Wilkinson, who runs Hollybush Farm Fellowship saw him, he called out, "Hey, look who is here! If it isn't our brother from Lincoln, August Ericson! Come up to the front here, brother, and give us a word of testimony!"

Going to Hollybush hadn't been August's first choice of an evening out, owing to the continual discomfort he was suffering with his hand. But if being there was bad, going up to the front like one of the walking wounded would be ten times worse!

He went, however.

To refuse would give his visitors a very wrong impression. As soon as he saw him make his way towards the platform, Jim Wilkinson enjoined him over the PA system, "I see you are wearing a bandage, August. Make sure you tell us what happened to your hand or arm or whatever it is."

On reaching the rostrum August gave a brief outline of the latest news from Sign Of The Fish. He had done this at Holly Bush before, and the congregation maintained a prayerful interest in the sanctified fish and chip shop. This was different, though, for the proprietor then proceeded to tell of the accident with the burning fat the previous afternoon, and how this was both causing him pain and would probably keep him off work for some six months.

He had no sooner finished his account than Jim announced, "This calls for prayer! We will pray for this man's healing. Stay where you are, August. We will ask your friends to come up and lay hands on you with some of our elders."

Suddenly, and it seemed from every angle, men began to appear. They surrounded the 'brother' with the big bandage, until he felt like a hooker in a rugby scrum. Every one of them reached forward to touch him at some point on his injured arm.

"Lord, You know this man's need," Jim Wilkinson prayed. "You know he works with his hands. Please give him a new hand, we beseech You." This was followed by a chorus of earnest 'Amens' from all over the building.

It seemed a tall order.

The skin had been burnt completely off August's hand in places.

When the prayer was over the scrum scattered just as suddenly and silently as it formed, and August returned to his seat.

It was a long run back to Lincoln later and everyone was exhausted when they returned. Dick and the boys had enjoyed their day and August had endured the most of it.

Having the healing of his hand prayed for in such a public manner in the evening had been a thrilling, but unexpected experience. Would anything out of the ordinary happen, though? That was the question.

Next morning it was back to the hospital as usual to have his dressing changed, and he continued to go there for almost a week.

On the Thursday morning, just a week after August's accident the nurse gave his hand a thorough examination. "These burns are healing unbelievably quickly," she remarked, obviously somewhat surprised. She could have had no knowledge of the Hollybush Farm prayer session, nor would she have had any faith in such 'religious fancies' even had she known about it.

It was the Bank Holiday the following weekend and on the Sunday morning August called in the Hospital to have his dressing changed as usual. He and Jill were stopping off at the Outpatient's Department on their way to the Grapevine Christian Rally on the Lincolnshire Showground.

Again the speed of the healing of August's hand caused some consternation amongst the medical staff. "This is amazing," another nurse told him, "but you are now ready to go without your sling."

Later, in the Grapevine gathering, surrounded by Christians who were singing the praises of the Lord with great gusto and utter sincerity, August examined the hand that was now open to the air for the first time in ten days. He could move it, turn it over, and manipulate his fingers. His hand was almost healed.

'Thank you Lord, for saving my soul,

Thank you Lord, for making me whole,

Thank You Lord, for giving to me,

Your great salvation so full so free,' he sang with more conviction than most.

Monday was a holiday, and on Tuesday August was back in Sign of the Fish.

So much for six months.

His accident had been twelve days previous.

The prayer session in Hollybush Farm Fellowship had been eleven days ago.

August's hand was still very tender and its skin was soft and sensitive, like that of a newborn baby.

But it worked.

And he was back where he was firmly convinced God wanted him to be.

Frying chips in Sign Of The Fish.

A FISHERMAN'S TALE

15 God had wonderful ways of proving His faithfulness to His Lincoln fish-fryer after he had relinquished his vision of big business. When August tearfully surrendered his personal aspirations to the Divine will he was humbled to see how the mighty power of God could be demonstrated in a small place.

The healing of his hand was followed by the transformation of the city centre over a period of time. One of the features of a realignment of the shopping streets of Lincoln was the establishment of a new city square just twenty five yards from the Sign Of The Fish restaurant at the end of Sincil Street. Then the street itself, with its four hundred year old buildings, was given a facelift. This included repainting, new paving and the introduction of a series of decorative planters at strategic points.

August, Jill and all the staff at Sign Of The Fish were intrigued to see a team of City Council workmen arriving one day with a pair of summer seats on the back of a lorry. These they bolted to a specially prepared base, just opposite the shop. Their seating capacity had just been enhanced by the provision of free seating for their take-away customers!

The reorganisation of the city centre led to an increase in business for Sign Of The Fish. The rejuvenation of his burnt hand demonstrated to August that God still had the power to heal His servants in His will.

How, though, could they further expand the influence and outreach of Sign Of The Fish without leaving the building? That was his main concern. He believed that God had revealed to him, and that rather painfully, that the answer did not lie in mobile vans, further shops, or diversification into innovative product such as home made pre-fried chips.

How then could it be done?

The solution came in a telephone call one day.

August had purchased most of the tracts for the toast racks on the tables from CPO, the Christian Publicity Organisation, from Worthing, Sussex. As the volume of customers through Sign Of The Fish had grown steadily over the years, and particularly after the changes to the city centre, so had the amount of tracts disappearing to be read. This in turn led to an increase in orders for material from CPO.

The man on the end of the line was Bob Bond from the publishing organisation. After the introductory pleasantries he came to the point of why he had rung.

"You seem to have a tremendous turnover of tracts and pamphlets through your shop, August," he began. "We here at CPO were wondering if you would be interested in having an attractive little booklet done giving a brief outline of your personal testimony and how you were led into the work you are doing now. It would be interesting, too, if we could tell of some of the spiritual harvest you have gleaned for God there."

"Yes, that could possibly be a good idea," August replied, with some hesitation. He had often contemplated having something local to attract the attention of customers, but it had never occurred to him that this could feature Sign Of The Fish. "That certainly would be topical. What would it entail?" he went on to enquire.

Pleased that his client appeared at least interested, Bob proceeded to give him a quick rundown on what would be required in the production of the booklet he had envisaged. August would have to write a brief synopsis of the high points of his life and service for the Lord. With that under way Bob would travel to Lincoln to see the work for himself.

There was one other question that August felt he had to ask. "How much would this cost us?" he was anxious to know.

Having anticipated such a question, Bob had done his sums and had the answer ready. He gave his prospective customer a rough estimate of the cost of such an ingenious enterprise in in-house literature evangelism, explaining that if the numbers of tracts ordered were larger they would become cheaper pro rata.

When he had made a note of Bob's suggested sequence of activities leading to the ultimate publication of a specially designed booklet, and the financial outlay involved, August asked for time to consider the matter.

He shared the idea with Jill and both of them brought it before the Lord in earnest prayer. After a week of constant communion with God and sharing with some of their closest Christian friends they decided to go ahead.

August phoned Bob to inform him of their decision and he arranged to come to Lincoln to see for himself what was happening.

In the meantime August embarked on something he had never done in his life to date. That was writing down his testimony. He had told it in meetings often, but had never attempted to condense what he said in an hour into about two thousand words before. He wrote down, tore up, and began again. When almost finished a further attempt he remembered something more, so he ripped up what he had done and began again.

He began again, many times.

When, after numerous abortive attempts, he had eventually finished his testimony to his satisfaction August realised that there was something he needed to add. It would be imperative that anyone reading his story should not be left in any doubt as to how they, too, could find the peace and joy which he enjoyed in life through having trusted in Jesus. So he added a clear outline of the Good News, or Gospel, to be included at the end, with a suggested précis prayer, which if uttered from the heart, would put the penitent soul in touch with God.

Since he had no experience of what was required in a piece of Christian writing, August was anxious to have his work reviewed by someone who had. Having reread his completed copy many times to make sure it was exactly as he wanted it, he forwarded it to Rev. David Pawson, who had once lived in Lincoln, but was by then residing in the south of England. He invited David to give him an honest opinion on it, suggesting any improvements that could be made.

In less than two weeks he had David's reply. 'This looks good to me, August,' he wrote back. 'There is nothing that I could add.'

Just as August was putting the finishing touches to the written account of his encounter with Christ, Bob Bond from CPO arrived in Lincoln. He stayed with the Ericson family at their home but went in with Jill and August to their work every day. Having taken part in the morning prayer and Bible study sessions before opening, he spent the remainder of the day in Sign Of the Fish. This allowed him to savour the Christian atmosphere of the place, while mingling and chatting with both customers and staff. Bob also took a number of photographs which he thought could prove useful in illustrating the proposed booklet.

With the writing done, and the photographs taken, there remained just the question of selecting an appropriate title for the would-be Gospel pamphlet. August discussed this matter with Jill,

Bob and some others and a number of ideas were put forward. When he had reflected on them all for some time, August felt drawn to the one he had thought of right at the beginning. What could better represent the life of a fisherman's son, who spent a high percentage of his working hours frying fish than, A Fisherman's Tale? It tied in too with an invitation of Jesus which he had been seeking to make one of his aims in life. 'Follow me and I will make you fishers of men,' his Lord had promised.

Bob returned to his office in Worthing with all the material required to produce a booklet on the life of August Ericson and the vision of Sign Of The Fish. And August returned to the busy round in the fish and chip shop where the possibility of such a publication gradually faded from his mind.

It was catapulted to the forefront of his consciousness again a few weeks later when a draft copy of a tract with the title A Fisherman's Tale arrived through the letterbox, complete with a graded price list and order form.

August and Jill read it over time and again, and then prayed for guidance once more. It was thrilling to see the mock-up of their tract, but now they were faced with another practical question. How many of them should they order?

Eventually they decided on the figure of five thousand. It seemed a lot at the time, but they believed that there was a need for this local testimony in their shop, and they had proved time and again in their Christian experience already that they served the God of miracles.

When the large carton containing five thousand copies of A Fisherman's Tale arrived by carrier three weeks later August experienced a strange mix of emotions. It gave him a glow of pleasure to see his life story attractively presented in print. On the other hand he felt humble as he began to wonder why CPO had chosen to feature his personal testimony and the saga of the Sign Of The Fish in a special edition tract.

He carried them down to the shop that morning and placed the opened box on the floor during the early morning staff prayer meeting. After the staff had been afforded the opportunity to see the tract, which many of them dived into reading straight away, they had a solemn, focused prayer session. Everyone prayed pointedly that God would bless this little booklet to their customers, and in a wider context, to all the citizens of Lincoln. The burden of their petition was that He, in His mighty power to save, would draw at least one soul to Himself as a result of it. If that happened they reckoned it would all have been worthwhile.

Then before opening time, and with what almost amounted to a sense of awe, they placed many copies of A Fisherman's Tale amongst the other tracts on the racks on the tables.

How would they be received? That was what everyone wondered.

In reverential silence, was the answer. For about three days Sign Of The Fish became more like a church than a chip shop. Everyone was reading.

People had barely time to look up to give their orders, they were so busy reading.

Plates were pushed away from places, with portions of deep-fried haddock half consumed and looking decidedly sad and mushy peas which had collapsed into a mushy mess. The customers who had ordered them had neither the time nor the interest to eat them.

They were too busy reading.

Virtually the only customers who dared to talk were talking to each other and the staff about 'the little book'.

Many asked permission before taking them away with them, assuring Jill or August or some other staff member that they knew somebody who 'would really love to read it.'

This was encouraging and an answer to prayer.

They would certainly have no difficulty in using up their initial order of five thousand copies.

What, though, of their prayer that someone would be brought to the Lord through reading it?

Could God use A Fisherman's Tale to make a fisherman's son who fried fish in The Sign Of The Fish a 'fisher of men' for His kingdom?

VAL

16

They hadn't long to wait for a response.

Less than four weeks after The Fisherman's Tale was placed prayerfully on the tables at Sign Of The Fish a letter arrived addressed to August and Jill.

Since neither of the recipients recognised either the handwriting or the postmark it stirred an immediate curiosity and generated a glow of excitement within them. Bills they disliked and circulars they discarded but this bulky and obviously personal letter lay beyond those boring brackets. Hopefully it would be in the relatively rare category which people subconsciously classify as 'highly desirable.'

When August slit it open and began to read he was moved. Tears came to his eyes, and the occasional 'Praise The Lord! Amen!' burst from his lips as he read,

'Dear Friends,

I came to Lincoln by chance two weeks ago and again by chance went for a meal in your café. While there I browsed through your booklets, **'A Fisherman's Tale,'** *and* **'Coming Home'**

On my way home I read them thoroughly and it made me realise for the first time that this is what I have been searching for. On my home-coming and since, I have been a totally different person, 'born again', content and at peace with the Lord. I have become a non-drinker of which I was a very heavy one. I asked our Lord to help me with this. I find I have energy to see to my home and family better than ever before, making them content and happy. Many years I have searched and now I have found someone and the love I feel for our Lord overwhelms me. I can feel my closeness to Him as I read His words in the Bible, which I can honestly say I have never read before in all the thirty-nine years of my life.

I am still in the early stages of learning so I am asking you to answer a few questions for me. The Lord gives me lots of answers to questions through reading His words which I study every day. I truly have faith in Him and all his works. Love and God bless,

Valerie.'

What a thrill! What excitement! What praise!

When August read the letter out at the prayer meeting before the opening of the shop the next morning everyone was delighted. God had answered their prayer, and a spontaneous session of expressed appreciation ensued. There was no holding back that morning!

August replied to Valerie's letter within days, posting off his response to an address in the London district of East Ham. He offered to try and answer any question that Valerie had about the Christian life, and encouraged her to keep in touch.

From her next letter August gathered that Val, as she signed herself the second time, had already made rapid strides in her faith. The recent convert had two pertinent questions for the fish-frying fisher of men, however.

Her first query was one which has often been raised by followers of the Lord Jesus. Indeed His original band of hand-picked disciples had problems with it. 'Lord, teach us to pray,' they implored their Master.

'I want to get close to God in prayer,' was Val's desire.

'Are there any special words I should use when I pray? Is there any particular pattern I should conform to so that I can be sure God pays attention to my prayers?' was the gist of her concern.

'How can I witness more effectively to my friends and neighbours?' was the second issue that seemed to be causing Val some heart-searching. 'I would love them all to discover the same satisfaction as I have found since I came to Jesus.'

August had led the staff at Sign Of The Fish in prayer that God would use the booklet 'A Fisherman's Tale' to the salvation of at least one soul. Now that had happened and he found himself assuming a completely new role, one which he hadn't really dared to anticipate. It was that of spiritual mentor to a new believer.

Recalling Stuart Bell's wise counsel in his life after he had come to the Saviour, and drawing upon his own experiences of the Lord since then, August answered Val's questions as best he could.

As they continued to correspond he realised that she was growing apace, not only as a Christian, but also as an evangelist. When he read her letters, both at home when he received them and then to the staff group before opening for the day, August became acutely aware that the lines of demarcation had all but disappeared. It had become difficult to decide as to who was actually counselling whom. If Val felt as challenged and inspired by his letters as he did by hers he would be doing well!

A miracle was taking place in East Ham and the more he heard of it the more the spiritual mentor from Lincoln longed to see it for himself. When Val invited him, in one of her letters, 'down to talk to our little group' he travelled south to London as soon as it could be arranged.

That first visit to Val's flat on a run-down estate was both a heartening and a humbling experience.

Treat number one was to meet Val. The skinny wisp of a woman claimed to be thirty-nine, but to someone who had never met her before she appeared more like fifty-nine. She confessed to having spent her life from late teenage hooked on drugs and dependent on alcohol. In her twenties she had been married to an abusive husband who beat her up from time to time when he just happened to have had more to drink than her. He had long since left her to her own devices, but all these facets of her former life had left their mark on her appearance.

What August noticed from the moment she opened the battered door of her flat to him was the light in her hollow sunken eyes. They seemed to flash with heavenly radiance. There was an unmistakeable sparkle about them. Val's life had been transformed and the proof of it danced in that twinkle in her eye. It was inescapable.

August hadn't been in the flat very long before others started to arrive, some carrying Bibles. Val greeted them, and then introduced them to her special guest one by one, in her broad Cockney accent. Two other men turned up with their wives, but the most of the people to attend that afternoon were women, who had walked there. They were obviously all from the immediate neighbourhood.

When the hostess was satisfied that everyone she had expected was present August was invited to speak to them. He hadn't time at that stage to marvel at this miraculous extension of the Sign Of The Fish, brought about by A Fisherman's Tale.

His audience were eagerly awaiting what he had to say.

He read a few verses from the Bible and began to comment on them. It wasn't long before he was interrupted by someone asking a question. As soon as he had satisfied that enquirer another question popped up from the opposite corner of the tightly packed living room. The question and answer session continued and as the group began to feel more at ease the discussions veered away from the passage the speaker had read and on to the practicalities of living out the Christian life on a housing estate in East Ham.

Some of the guests, who ranged in age from fifteen to fifty, had just recently been led to the Lord by Val's tireless witness. They were new babes in Christ with an insatiable thirst for the 'sincere milk of the Word' and a burning passion to share their faith with others.

As afternoon wore on into evening and nobody made any attempt to go home, August began to wilt, but his audience showed no signs whatsoever of easing off. He had travelled one hundred and forty miles to be with them, and was tired from the journey. Most of them had walked there with their Bibles, their questions and their genuine love for the Lord. There could be no stopping.

They had so much for which they wanted to praise God.

And they were unbelievably eager to learn more and more about Him.

Discussions were suspended briefly at the sound of sirens outside. Somebody had set a car on fire about fifty metres from the flat. Val let August and one or two others take a look out to see what was going on. The remainder didn't even trouble to rise from where they were sitting. That sort of thing was 'run of the mill' stuff for them. Soon Val had shown the firewatchers back to their seats. It was more important to her that they were all on fire for God.

Just after ten o'clock Val opened the front door of her flat to allow the first of her guests to leave and begin their homeward journey. As they had been engaged in animated conversation Val's vibrant study group had been able to ignore their immediate surroundings. When the door was opened, though, the din from downstairs exploded into the flat in all its fury, having echoed up the concrete corridors.

"They are having a bit of a party down there tonight," Val announced, unperturbed. "It will likely go on for most of the night!"

She was right, too. It did.

Not that August was too worried for he knew that if he was in the company of Val and some of her friends who were staying overnight, he would be safe. They knew the scene. And they also knew the Lord.

Val's love for her Saviour, and for the lives and souls of her friends and neighbours, was irrepressible. As August sat listening to her telling story after story of others she was witnessing to about Jesus he just felt like weeping all the time.

The staff at Sign Of The Fish had prayed so earnestly that God would save someone through 'A Fisherman's Tale'.

The only reason that he would ever want to leave Val's mission headquarters in East Ham, and return to Lincoln would be to tell Jill and the rest how those prayers had been answered.

If God never brought anybody else to Himself through 'A Fisherman's Tale' Val would have been worth every ounce of effort and every penny of expense that had been geared towards its production.

For she, with her fearless, fervent witness, was on her way to seeing dozens brought to Christ!

BOB, THE SAUSAGE MAN

17 Sign of the Fish was open for business twenty hours per week. Saturday was the busiest day, when they were open five hours, and the other days, Monday through to Friday, it was three hours over lunchtime. In this time hundreds of fish suppers were served and dozens of Fisherman's Tales were taken away to be read.

Thanks largely to Jill's affable nature and relaxed style of management August and she had managed to establish an excellent rapport with many of their regular customers. When reflecting upon why they had opened the café in the first place, however, they were aware that they had an even more important duty to discharge to these people, many of whom they saw three or four times every week, than merely supplying them with a reasonable and appetising meal, and a welcome cup of tea. They needed to hear about the Bread of Life for soul satisfaction and the living water which had the capacity to quench spiritual thirst forever.

Having given the matter some consideration and shared it with the staff at prayer times, August and Jill decided to hold an occasional fish and chip supper evening for these regulars. At this event all those invited would be served with a free fish and chip meal, but there would be more. When everybody had eaten someone would play a guitar and sing a few gospel pieces and one or two of the staff members would be asked to share a testimony.

One of the most encouraging contacts of those special supper evenings was a man called Bob. The staff had a nickname they used amongst themselves for this grumpy old clock and watch repairer. His particular preference for a certain Sign Of The Fish speciality had earned him the title of 'Bob, the sausage man'. Bob had come originally from the Lincolnshire fens, but had worked most of his life in the city, where he lived in splendid isolation in a prefab on the outskirts. Having lived a very frugal life Bob was ultra careful with his money which he kept zipped up and counted carefully in a little purse in his pocket. He always knew how much he had in that precious purse and there was never a penny escaped out of it without due deliberation.

So the prospect of a free meal proved altogether too tempting for Bob to resist.

He had his own particular views on the remainder of the carefully planned programme for the evening and had aired them to the staff when agreeing to come along.

"I will go for the free grub," he conceded, as though doing everyone a great favour. "But I am not in the slightest bit interested in Jesus and all this religious stuff you keep going on about." His acceptance speech was an amusing mix of reluctant appreciation and restrained aggression.

However reluctantly he had come, though, that evening Bob had a strange experience.

He had enjoyed his fish and chip supper as usual, and when the short session of testimony and Christian witness came to an end the friends from all around him began to leave. Perhaps they had babysitters in or elderly relatives to look after, but Bob was in no hurry home. He lived alone and was quite content to remain in the company for as long as possible.

A column of chatting companions had made its way in single file down the narrow stairs before Bob decided that it was probably time for him to bring up the rear. And it was then that something remarkable happened.

When he attempted to rise from his seat Bob couldn't move!

He had been troubled with arthritis for many years and just at that moment a cramping, crippling pain had seized him in both legs. His piercing cry of anguish brought Di, a staff member who had been tidying up a recently vacated table nearby, to his side.

"What's the matter, Bob?" she enquired, sympathetically.

"It's my legs!" came the agonised response. "I can't move them! And I can't get up from here!"

When she had spoken quietly to him for a few minutes to help him over the initial shock of his immobility Di went on to ask him, "Bob, do you mind if I pray with you?"

"I don't care what you do, duck!" Bob exclaimed in his rich Lincolnshire accent. All his former reservations about religion had obviously been dispelled in his desperation. "If you think it will do any good go ahead. Pray away!"

Having received the all clear Di rose from her seat beside him before he could change his mind, and placing her hands gently on Bob's shoulders, began to pray for him. The agonised outbursts ceased as her prayer seemed to soothe his immediate distress, but it had also ascended into the presence of an Almighty God.

On finishing her prayer Di resumed her seat and carried on chatting calmly. Sensing perhaps an easing in the pains in his legs Bob began to shuffle his feet about on the floor as he talked.

In less than five minutes he had placed his hands firmly on the table and begun to push himself up gingerly. He had the appearance of a man who was almost afraid to put pressure on his legs in case they would either cause him excruciating pain, or else buckle below him. As he rose more confidently to his feet an expression of utter amazement swept across his face.

"It's gone!" he exclaimed. "The pain's gone!"

Then with typical candour, and without any prompting from Di or any of the others he proceeded to what seemed to him the next logical step.

"If Jesus has done this, I want Jesus!" he announced, unashamedly. As soon as he had sat down again Di assumed the mantle of counsellor once more. This time it wasn't counsel on patience in the endurance of pain she was imparting, though. It was on the way of salvation, of how Christ had died for Bob on a cross. If he accepted Jesus into his life, which is what he claimed he wanted to do, then he could be free from the penalty of his sins forever.

While Di was engaged in conversation with Bob, the remainder of the staff were carrying on with their clearing up and cleaning up duties, praying fervently for this crotchety customer whom they had all come to respect. No one was ever sure whether they liked him because of, or in spite of, all his individual traits of character.

Their prayers were answered, for within fifteen minutes, Bob the sausage man had given his life to Christ.

The change that decision made in Bob's life was plain for all to see. The short-tempered, impetuous little man became even-tempered and patient. The rough, gruff huffy attitude had gone. Bob had become a completely new person. Friends who had known him all his life often exclaimed. "It can't be the same man!"

Although sixty-four years of age when he became a Christian, God had a wonderful blessing in store for his new child. After his conversion Bob began attending the New Life Christian Fellowship in Lincoln, and in less than a year he had overcome a lifelong fear of water to be baptised by immersion.

Mike Maguire, who had been working at Sign of The Fish when Bob was saved, was also a member of the New Life Christian Fellowship. He and his wife, Mary, took a special interest in the recent convert, helping to encourage him in his newly found faith.

As part of that ministry of support Bob became a frequent and welcome visitor to Mike and Mary's little home in the 'up the hill' end of Lincoln, near the cathedral. He had never thought that life could be any sweeter than it had become since he had trusted in Jesus, but in Mike and Mary's little front room one evening it took another turn for the better. The icing was about to be added to his cake of contentment.

Mary had asked Elsie, a lady from the Fellowship, who was both deaf and partially sighted, to share that particular evening with Mike, Bob and her. Elsie had responded to the invitation gladly, for although she lived in a dark, quiet world, she just loved company, and especially the company of other Christians.

The host and hostess were amazed at what happened that night. When the pair who had always been separated at Church by rows of seats, Elsie's inability to communicate, and Bob's inbuilt rural reticence, met, in the carefree closeness of that cosy room, there appeared to be an immediate, invisible bond between them.

For Bob, the shy one, it was love at first sight.

For Elsie, who wasn't quite so bashful, it was love at first touch. When she had reached out to hold Bob's hand, she just held on!

Although unable to hear , Elsie had learnt to speak, and she whispered to Mary on the way out, "That's the man for me!"

And he was. For Bob, as it so happened, felt that he too had met someone with whom he felt unusually at ease. She was also somebody he could help in a special way.

Jill and August joined Mike and Mary and a few other family friends at a simple wedding ceremony in the New Life Christian Fellowship some six months later. Elsie had procured a new cream dress for the occasion and Bob showed up all dressed up in the good suit he had bought for 'going to church' after his conversion.

Bob 'the sausage man' had found complete satisfaction, both of soul and in life. God had provided him, not only with the joy of

His salvation but also with one of His children as a partner by way of a bonus.

Just after the wedding Bob retired from his job as a watchmaker. He had now signed up for another full-time position, which was to provide him with untold pleasure.

He devoted himself to perfecting a unique touch and sign method of communicating with, and for, his new wife.

Bob had become eyes and ears to his beloved Elsie.

THAT THEY MIGHT HAVE LIFE

18

It was late on a sultry summer afternoon. August was returning to his car after a day in Sign Of The Fish when he saw a woman he knew sitting on one of a series of seats by the riverside. He was about to pass on with a cheery greeting when he realised that the lady on the seat looked rather upset. It was obvious that she had been crying.

"What's the matter, Susan?" August enquired sympathetically, stopping in his step. "Can I help?"

"Oh I doubt if you could help," the worried woman replied. "It's to do with my work, August. As you probably know I am involved with Life, an anti-abortion advisory group. Our present landlord has told us that we must vacate our office by the end of the month and we have nowhere else to go." She paused for a soft sniffle before concluding, "It almost seems sometimes as if the devil is winning."

This set August thinking.

There were two rooms surplus to immediate requirements on the top floor of the Sign Of The Fish building in Lincoln city centre. One of these rooms was used for storage, the other as a staff room. There was a lot of unused space in each. Their functions could easily be combined and carried out from either, leaving one vacant and available for use.

Having given Susan time to share a summary of the aims and activities of the Life organisation, and her apparently shattered vision for the future, August remained silent for a few minutes.

Both he and Susan stared blankly at the swans gliding gracefully about on the river. There was a silent serenity in shared sorrow.

"Although you said you didn't think I could help, you could just have been wrong there," August broke the silence to make a suggestion at length. "I will give you my telephone number for I believe that there is possibly something I could do to help out. I will need to think it through, though. If the local branch organisers are interested ask them to give me a ring."

Susan took a note of the number and, smiling for the first time in the entire conversation, remarked with an air of confidence, "I will be surprised if you don't hear from them."

Her assessment of the situation had been spot on.

August had a call from the area manager of Life two days later asking if they could meet as soon as possible. A suitable time was arranged and August went to see the district director of the organisation anxious to learn more about their work locally, and help if possible.

As he heard the validated figures of the numbers of unborn babies who had been, to use the director's description, 'murdered, in the Lincoln area over the past year alone, August was shocked. He had no idea that the problem was so widespread.

Upon enquiring what they would be using his top floor room for, if granted, August was informed that it would be an advisory centre. Pregnant young women would be counselled there as to the moral unacceptability, and possible physical after effects to the mother, of abortion. Their office would provide more than a platform for sounding off on ethical issues, however. Girls would be advised of the alternatives to abortion and support would be offered to allow them to have and rear their babies naturally.

When he heard the objectives of the Life movement explained to him so simply, and accompanied by such stark statistics, August readily agreed terms for the use of an upstairs room as an office and counselling centre. In the hours that Sign Of The Fish was open for the sale of fish and chips that small space could become a sanctuary of support and guidance to anyone caring to visit it.

On the day the office opened for business a small plaque bearing the simple, single word, 'LIFE', was fixed to the wall outside the Sincil Street café. That word often struck August with a particular poignancy as he hurried in past it for the morning prayer session before opening. His Saviour had declared that His purpose in coming to earth was 'that they might have life, and that they might have it to the full.' Surely the preservation of physical life in unborn babies was an appropriate adjunct to the proclamation of spiritual life through faith in Jesus Christ to maturing adults.

As the weeks went on the value of this work, and of his decision to allow it to be carried on upstairs, was confirmed to him. Often in the middle of busy lunch hour periods the chief fish fryer would catch fleeting glimpses of young women, who were not Sign of The Fish customers, hurrying up the narrow stairs.

This initial, marginal involvement with the issue caused August to embark upon a further examination of the anti-abortion argument. The more he researched the more incensed he became at what he considered as a violation of God's creation of 'a living soul.'

Eventually he decided to do something about it. But what could a particularly non-violent, inoffensive owner of a fish restaurant in Lincoln do to highlight the plight of the unborn potential murder victim?

August considered the matter carefully for a few weeks and then a plan began to formulate in his fertile brain. He could write to people in high places drawing attention to the issue as dramatically as possible.

That was it! He would draft a letter and send it to Her Majesty The Queen, every member of the House of Commons, every member of the House of Lords, every leading churchman, every consultant gynaecologist and obstetrician in the country... The list lengthened every time he thought of it. There were so many people, and if a small percentage of them a few of them took even a midget step to further the cause it would all be worthwhile.

That letter took weeks to compose. August became obsessed with it. He was constructing, and then immediately redrafting, impactive sentences when driving the car, walking the dog or preparing mushy peas. He drew references from the Bible, illustrations from life and authenticated statistics from reputable sources. The whole letter was revamped dozens of times. If he were going to send a letter to all the personages he had planned, it would have to be impressive. It would be vitally important to achieve the maximum effect with the minimum of words.

With his letter almost complete August found himself confronting a very practical problem. Expense. The printing, preparation and posting of the letter he had drafted, to all the people he had envisaged, would require an appreciable amount of money. Could he justify that expenditure?

The pace of progress slowed considerably as August began to contemplate the matter seriously. He prayed earnestly that God would grant him a definite sign that he should proceed with his massive mail shot.

This confirmation came from an unexpected source, at a most unexpected time, within the next few weeks.

August and Jill had travelled with some friends to hear one of their favourite Gospel singing groups, Second Chapter Of Acts, perform at a concert in Birmingham. During the course of the concert, and in an interval between numbers, a member of the band dropped a single remark. It came totally out of the blue and was not connected in any way to anything that had preceded it, nor could it have been construed as an introduction to what was to follow.

"How do you think Jesus feels," she asked the capacity audience pointedly, "when a baby is aborted?"

As thousands pondered the possible solution to that problem August reckoned that if anyone else responded positively to that challenge it would be an added extra. As far as he was concerned that question had been mooted by Divine direction to spur him on to taking the next critical step in his postal abortion-awareness campaign.

He retuned from Birmingham to Lincoln that night, totally convinced that God was guiding him to send out his carefully composed letter to as many public figures as possible. He would begin at once. The only remaining obstacle to be overcome was that of obtaining the hundreds of addresses he would need to make the venture viable.

Her Majesty the Queen's wasn't hard to come by, and those of both members of the Houses of Parliament proved only slightly more difficult. Finding the addresses of every consultant gynaecologist and obstetrician in the country, however, proved to be a much more onerous task. August prayed for guidance and persevered on the telephone until he was satisfied that this goal had also been achieved.

When the letters were eventually posted with the address of Sign Of The Fish, 42 Sincil Street, Lincoln as their headline August prayed specifically for a dual outcome. He asked God that He would use them to the awakening of someone to the moral implications and possible physical and emotional side effects of abortion. Having quoted a number of well-known verses from the Gospel of John in the text of the letter he also prayed that somebody would have a personal encounter with God after reading it.

Soon the postman in Sincil Street began to wonder at the increase in the volume of mail for number 42. He had now often handfuls of letters to deliver, rather than the usual trickle of windowed envelopes containing probably unwelcome bills.

August had no idea that his simple letter, which contained nothing more than a firmly held moral and spiritual conviction, could invoke such a vitriolic response in some. These people reacted very bitterly, their consciences obviously stung by the startling statistics and scriptural quotations included. A few razor-edged replies even went so far as to include veiled threats to the sender.

There were a number of encouraging acknowledgements too, though, many of these from churchmen. Some leading Bishops wrote letters commending August for his Christian courage in embarking upon his postal campaign, but the reply that he treasured most didn't come from a church dignitary. It arrived in the company of a few others less uplifting one morning from the father of a gynaecologist. This letter was so special because it helped vindicate all the trouble and expense associated with the project.

The elderly gentleman wrote to thank August for his letter and to report that his son had been challenged into action by it, on two different counts. One of these was spiritual, the other professional.

This middle-aged consultant, who had asked Jesus into his heart as a boy but had backslidden in his faith, was restored to the Lord as a result of reading August's letter. And that wasn't all, either! He had also taken the bold decision not to perform any more abortions unless they could be totally justified on medical grounds.

August rejoiced when he read that.

He had no idea how many infant lives had been saved through the counselling that had taken place upstairs in Sign Of The Fish, and there must have been many. Now he had this letter in his hand to prove that his postal targeting campaign had been used of God to influence the life of at least one influential person.

And that was enough.

That was all he had asked of God, and the threatened unborn of His creation would undoubtedly benefit in the years to come.

Or in the words of Jesus, 'I have come that they might have *life.'*

19 IT'S JUST THE HAPPY BACCY, DARLIN'

August and Jill always afforded themselves at least a few days free from frying during the summer to attend the Dales Bible Week, held in a marquee in the Showgrounds in Harrogate, Yorkshire. One year when there they skipped the Friday evening rally to go across to the Hollybush Farm Christian Fellowship in Northallerton. Jim Wilkinson had made them promise, virtually every time they were in contact, that they would 'drop in any time you are up this way, and update us on what is happening at Sign Of The Fish.'

On arriving there they were warmly welcomed and Jim asked August to share a short testimony with them. He was to 'tell something of how it all began for those who haven't heard the story, and then give us all the most recent information on what is going on.'

He did as instructed, relating all the very latest encouraging aspects of the work in Lincoln. The tale of Bob the sausage man stimulated the enthusiastic audience into producing a spontaneous chorus of 'Amen's laced with the occasional 'Praise the Lord!'

When the meeting was over a man whom August had never met before approached him. The stranger introduced himself as Randolph Pooley from The Full Gospel Businessman's Fellowship in Bude, Cornwall.

"That was wonderful, brother," he went on. "I was wondering if you would feel free to come and speak at our annual dinner of the Full Gospel Businessmen's Fellowship International in Bude in September?"

August found that he was free on the date suggested, and agreed to go.

The Granada had long since gone, and August set out on the day of the dinner in the old banger which had become the Ericson's only car. He had studied maps carefully before setting out and had allowed himself ample time to make the cross-country journey from Lincoln to north Cornwall.

Everything was fine and August was driving along organising his thoughts for the after-dinner speech he would be expected to make when the car suddenly lost power and spluttered to a halt. He had reached the Exeter by-pass, but was still some fifty miles from Bude.

It was five o'clock, and right in the middle of rush hour.

When he was convinced that repairing the recalcitrant car was out of the question, August just bowed his head in it and prayed, "Lord, I can't let these people down. They are expecting me as Your servant. Please show me how to get to Bude."

With that he locked up the broken-down vehicle, turned his back on it, and began to hitchhike. He had never been reduced to 'thumbing a lift' before, but now felt that it was his only option.

Two lifts whisked August away from the bustle of traffic around Exeter and deposited him in a narrow Cornish country road with sharp bends and high banks topped with even higher hedges. It seemed as though he had been miraculously transported, in a matter of minutes, from the hurly burly of city life and the mad rush of motorways, into the very heart of 'England's green and pleasant land'.

August had no time to relax and enjoy this idyllic rural retreat, however.

His sole concern was reaching Bude for half-past seven, and time was marching on. Having walked along that desolate country road for ten minutes without ever seeing a vehicle of any sort August was encouraged to hear the sound of a tractor approaching. The chances of the driver being on his way to Bude were slim the totally lost traveller reckoned, but he might at least be able to give him directions.

As the tractor drew almost level with him, August flagged it down. "How far is it to Bude from here?" he yelled up at the driver over the growl of the engine.

"It's more than twenty miles," came the driver's reply as he leant down out of the cab to make himself heard.

"Well please can you point me to the right road to take me there?" August went on, his mounting anxiety and frustration beginning to waver through into his voice. "I'm supposed to be speaking at a dinner there at seven thirty."

"Oh so you are the speaker then," the Cornishman's face creased into a welcoming smile as though he had been expecting 'the speaker' to turn up on his remote farm all day. "I'm going to that dinner too. Hop up on the back there. I'm just on my way home to clean up. Then we can both go together!"

August heaved a great sigh of relief before clambering stiffly up behind the driver "Thank you Lord!" he kept repeating softy as he swayed gently in an attempt to maintain his balance as they roared back to the farmhouse. "Thank you for answering my prayers! I was lost but Jesus found me! Amen! Thank you Lord!"

When August and his farmer friend were late in arriving at the dinner in Bude it was difficult to distinguish who was the more relieved, the speaker or the organiser. Randolph Pooley had spent an anxious few minutes wondering if the man from Lincoln was going to turn up at all.

He had appeared though, and the evening was a great success. The audience was enthralled with August's fascinating testimony of implicit faith in God. A gratifying result of that one engagement in Bude was that August received further opportunities to glorify God in the sharing of his story all over mainland Britain.

With the constantly developing saga of Sign Of The Fish and the Fisherman's Tale being widely appreciated at home August was afforded a unique opportunity to share his story on the other side of the Atlantic. Stuart Bell, who had developed an extensive preaching ministry, asked his friend if he would consider accompanying him on a preaching tour of Pennsylvania, USA.

When Dick Heaney, the pastor from Pennsylvania who had being staying with the Ericson family at the time of the healed hand incident heard of the proposed trip he arranged an interesting encounter for the English visitor. August was asked to give a personal testimony in the State Penitentiary in Philadelphia.

As he walked along what seemed to be at least half a mile of corridor in the massive prison with Dick and a couple of the guards August's stomach turned over with fear. On either side of him huge, surly, coloured men stared blankly out of their cells. Are these the guys that will be in my meeting? he wondered. If one of those blokes turns on me he'll kill me!

At the end of the long walk August was ushered into a large room. It was filled with more of these muscular men sitting around muttering to one another under the watchful eye of a number of guards.

August was welcomed and told that he would have up to forty-five minutes to speak. Having prayed silently, but fervently, for guidance, August stood up. Words came slowly out of a dried up mouth at the start, but as he realised that most of the prison inmates were listening intently they began to flow more easily. God seemed to guide him as to what to say and how to say it.

When his time was up, and he sat down again, August felt physically and emotionally drained. It had all been worth it, though. His message had been both appreciated by the crowded congregation and blessed by God. Two men waited behind and told Dick that they had committed their lives to the Lord at the end of August's address. And the man who had organised the meeting, a former Mafia enforcer but now a gentle Christian, came to him with a further invitation. It was one he cherished because of who it came from, but would be unable to fulfil for practical reasons.

"That was wonderful, man," he began. "Would you like to come back and talk to us again next month?"

He wasn't long home from his American trip until Jill informed her husband that they had received an invitation that they could, and would be accepting. It was to Val's wedding.

The energetic personal evangelist from East Ham was marrying Roy, whom she had led to the Lord through her persistent and consistent witness some months before.

It was a lovely wedding. The couple, whose lives had both been transformed by the love of Christ were obviously very much in love with one another.

At the reception, though, August began to wonder at Val's choice of guests.

A table of twelve, not far from where Jill and he were seated, appeared particularly noisy. They were passing cigarettes around and laughing in a boisterous, blasé manner. Imagine asking a crowd like that along to a Christian wedding, he thought.

When the new bride was making her round of the tables August nodded across to the merrymakers and remarked, "They seem to be having a good time over there."

"Aye, they are indeed," Val replied, totally unfazed. "It's just the happy baccy y' know, darlin'."

'The happy baccy.' Val's guests were smoking marijuana at her wedding reception!

As Val left them to speak to the revellers at the adjoining table August changed his mind about the hostess and her choice of guests. A sense of respect seemed to fall over the table as she approached it. It was obvious that everyone there held the new bride in high esteem, not for the person she once was, but for the person she had recently become, through faith in Christ.

A scripture verse shot into August's mind. It was, 'This man receives sinners, and eats with them'. How foolish he had been to question Val's integrity in who she invited to her wedding. This is just the kind of place Jesus would have been! Among the sinners, eating with them!

Val had seen more people contacted for Christ since her conversion than he had in half a lifetime. She, though, had come to the Lord, through A Fisherman's Tale in Sign Of The Fish.

August was at a loss to know whether to laugh or cry. Whether to shout 'Hallelujah!' or pray, 'Lord, forgive me!' For he ranged from feeling thrilled to feeling chastened in almost equal measures as he watched Val move from table to table, and from person to person, unashamedly sharing her faith.

A few months after Val's wedding August was the guest speaker at the Full Gospel Businessmen's International Conference in Malvern, Worcestershire one Saturday. At the end of the morning session a well-dressed gentleman came up to him and announced with a friendly mock-formalism, "My name is Wyn Severn. I claim you in the name of the Lord to come to California. If you do I will arrange meetings for you in and around Los Angeles, including Santa Ana at the Demos Shakarian Home Chapter'. To complete the ceremony, and to publicly stake his 'claim', Wyn, as he had introduced himself, fixed an American flag pin into the momentarily mystified speaker's lapel.

August was on his way to America, again, though not just immediately.

It was in the summer of 1990 that August was at last free to take Wyn up on his invitation and he and daughter Emma set off for California. Emma had trusted in Jesus as a little girl of seven, had always had an ambition to visit America, and had achieved creditable grades in her 'A' levels at school after a period of prolonged and intensive study. Taking all these factors into account her dad deemed her to be the ideal travelling companion for this trip to the USA.

The tour went well with many memorable meetings but the event which had the most lasting impact on the fish-fryer far from home occurred early one morning on the way to Pasadena. Emma and August had been stopping with a lovely lady called Anna, away out in the desert, and Emma loved it there.

When she heard that her dad was leaving early that morning to drive to Pasadena to do a radio broadcast she opted to stay behind. The prospect of a long journey with nothing much to do at the end of it didn't appeal to her. So dad set out alone.

Having left without breakfast August stopped at a roadside stall and purchased a hoagie. On his earlier visit to the States August had become fond of that North American speciality, the hoagie, which was nothing more, or less, than half a yard of bread stuffed with cheese, ham or salad in any mixture of the customer's choice.

It was a calm, warm early morning and August had pulled in at the roadside to enjoy his hoagie when the car suddenly jolted forward two or three feet. Assuming that someone had rammed him from behind, August hopped out of the car as quickly as he could, hoagie in hand.

But there was nobody there!

The long straight road stretched away empty and deserted in both directions until it disappeared into the shimmering haze that had become the horizon.

He climbed back into the driver's seat and sat listening to the radio while he went on eating. Suddenly a voice cut in to say that the Los Angeles area had been hit by an earthquake measuring 6.5 on the Richter scale. So *that* was what had caused his car to jolt forward. An earthquake!

Assuming that the earthquake was far from where he was August finished his hoagie and proceeded to Pasadena. When he drove into the city, however, he realised just how serious the earthquake had been. Water poured from fractured mains and the road was littered with all kinds of masonry and debris.

Having followed the detailed directions he had been given August managed to negotiate all the obstacles on his route and arrive at the building in which the broadcasting station was housed, at the appointed time. Still following his instructions he went up four floors in the elevator to be met by his host and escorted into the studio.

Before the broadcasting team began explaining the procedure to their guest speaker August asked if they could have a time of prayer together. He could see that the technicians were not used to such requests in the middle of a busy day, but they complied with their visitor's request.

Then, as they stood together in a circle, holding hands and asking God's blessing on the broadcast-to-be the whole building was rocked with an after shock of the 'quake.

August was excited when the prayer session finished. "That was just like what happened to the early church in Acts four," he remarked to his host. "You remember it says that when they had prayed the place where they were meeting was shaken. God is going to bless this broadcast, I believe."

When all the last minute checks had been completed August gave his testimony and shared the word of the Lord over the radio.

"There you are Mr. Ericson," the host said when the broadcast was finished. "Your story of Sign Of The Fish has now gone out into China! And I believe you are right. God is going to bless it."

On his way down in the elevator later August felt exhilarated.
He had experienced the mighty power of God in creation that
day, and thousands, perhaps millions, in China, had heard the story
of Sign Of The Fish.

August was on a spiritual 'high'. Feeling God's power, doing
God's will and sharing God's Word were how he got his kicks.

They were his 'happy baccy'!

IT'S NOT MY BUSINESS

20

It was obvious that the young couple had weighty matters on their minds.

They had waited behind to speak to August after a Full Gospel Businessmen's Fellowship meeting in Lancashire. When he had bade all those on their way home a casual 'Goodnight' August sat down with them to find out if there was any way in which he could help.

'I'm Peter, and this is my wife, Donna," the well-groomed young man broke the ice with an introduction, "and we live in Rawtenstall, near Burnley. We have just come to know the Lord about six months ago and were both moved by your story of Sign Of The Fish. It was how you handed it over to the Lord, and tried to run it for Him, that really impressed us."

Peter looked sideways at his wife who seemed fairly well advanced in a pregnancy, for approval, before continuing. Assured by her shy smile he went on, "I am a director in a firm that manufactures furniture, and Donna works in the company office. We would love to run our business for God, in the same way as you did with your fish and chip shop, but unfortunately my business partner is not a Christian. So what do you think we should do? We just long to put the Lord Jesus first in every aspect of our lives, including our business."

"That's wonderful," August began his reply with a few words of encouragement. It was difficult to advise a couple he had just met a few minutes before, on such complex issues. "God always honours those who honour Him, and I know from experience that it is a big thing, but an extremely rewarding thing, to hand a business totally over to Him."

The matter of the non-Christian partner would have to be dealt with first, though, and in that regard August had no other option but to refer the young couple to the Scriptures. "The problem is that you can't hand a business over to God when you have a non-Christian partner who probably wouldn't want to do that, nor would he understand why you would want to do it. It would be best if that partnership could be dissolved, even over a space of time. I appreciate that this could be a problem but Paul warned the Christians in Corinth when he was writing to them in his second epistle, chapter six and verse fourteen, not to be 'unequally yoked together with unbelievers'."

After some further discussion and a short time of prayer, August left Peter and Donna, promising to pray for them, and to keep in contact.

There were many counselling sessions over the telephone in the months that were to follow. It seemed that from the moment Peter decided to try and run a business for God everything that could go wrong did go wrong. Satan appeared to resent the idea and showed himself both willing and able to oppose it at every opportunity.

One of the company's major customers went into liquidation owing them a substantial sum of money which it would prove almost impossible to recoup. Then when Peter's partner and he did agree to split up it was in the middle of an economic recession. God had answered one of August and Peter's prayers, but business was at a low ebb. Expensive, top quality leather lounge suites were not high on everybody's shopping list at that time. Workers all over the country were losing their jobs, and people were more concerned with buying groceries than luxury goods.

August travelled up from Lincoln to Peter and Donna's factory in Rawtenstall to advise them on more than one occasion. He found it both touching and thrilling to see another business beginning the day as he and Jill had determined to do in Sign Of The Fish. Before a machine was started up, or a piece of leather was cut or stitched in that factory Peter and Donna gathered the staff into a large office and read the Bible and prayed with them.

Although the young company director and his wife were determined to acknowledge God and afford Him pole position in their lives this did not mean that He was going to allow them to lead the race on every lap. It seemed that He was prepared to test them on every bend. He had done it with Job, in the Bible, one of the first men ever to believe in Him, so long ago. Now it was happening to Peter.

The flow of orders began to dry up. The books were empty. The future looked bleak.

How could he go on?

Why was God allowing this to happen to him?

Could a business that had been carefully and conscientiously managed and monitored, and wholly and whole-heartedly dedicated to God, fail?

It was beginning to look that way. And it caused August grave concern, for he felt in part responsible for encouraging the enthusiastic young Christian couple to go it alone with God.

He prayed earnestly for them. He shared it with his staff at the morning prayer times in Sign Of The Fish and they began to pray too. Christian workers in a business that was at that moment running fairly smoothly for God in Lincoln had begun to pray for the staff in another business that looked like running into the buffers, for God, nearly one hundred miles away.

When it appeared that things couldn't get any worse, they did.

Demand dried up completely.

No new orders had come in for weeks.

Peter and Donna hit rock bottom.

What were they to do now? Next?

One Monday morning after a sleepless night and a half-eaten breakfast, Peter went out for a walk. He climbed up the gentle hill behind his house and gazed down at the town below him, kick-starting itself into another working week.

His sole purpose in that early morning stroll was to share his deep concerns with the Lord in solitude. "It's all in Your hands now, Lord," he cried out in anguish as he walked along. "We have done all we can but we have no more work coming in. We can probably manage this week, but unless something wonderful happens we won't be able to pay the wages at the end of next week. Please help us, Lord. Show us Your will. Show us Your way."

Shortly after that Peter and Donna set off for the factory, had their usual prayer session with the staff, and then went about their daily duties. They had heavy hearts. How were they going to tell a skilled and loyal workforce that they were soon to lose their jobs?

It was well on in the morning when the telephone rang. "Hello," the obviously foreign voice began, "I am a furniture buyer from Holland and I am at Manchester airport at the moment. Could I possibly come and see your goods?"

Peter was glad of anyone coming to do a factory tour, and when the Dutchman arrived by taxi in mid-afternoon he duly showed him around. Before he left he asked for a price list and catalogue. His parting promise before returning to his waiting taxi was, "I will speak to my partners in Holland and I will contact you again."

"That will be fine. Thank you very much," Peter replied, but the taxi probably hadn't reached the airport before he had dismissed it from his mind. If he had a pound for every empty promise he had been given, he wouldn't be in his present situation.

The Dutch buyer proved more reliable than many, though. A week later he phoned again to ask if he could bring some colleagues from his company along to see Peter's factory and the high quality furniture he was producing.

Peter and Donna were pleased at this development and a few days later the Dutch delegation arrived. They toured the factory, inspected the product, and asked endless questions.

Having satisfied themselves that they had seen all they wanted to see and learnt all they needed to know, they returned to the office to give their verdict. As they sat surrounded by the promotional material Peter had given them and the scribbled notes they had made themselves, the man who had been the original contact spoke up on behalf of all of them.

"If we were to place an order with you today could you provide us with thirty suites by the first of next month?" he enquired.

Peter's heart fluttered and he swallowed hard. 'By the first of next month.' That gave him a little over three weeks. Trying to disguise a mixture of rapture and relief he replied in his best, matter-of-fact, business voice, "Yes. I'm sure that would be possible. It may mean putting some of the men on overtime but we can do it."

A price was agreed and an order form filled out. Then, since it was an export order, the account had to be settled ahead of delivery. The senior partner of the visiting group produced a chequebook and made out a payment to Peter's company for the full amount. In advance!

The party left soon afterwards to catch a flight back home and Peter sat in his office with the cheque before him. "Thank You, Lord," he whispered softly.

That initial order was fulfilled as agreed, before the first of the next month, and another followed it. Soon the Dutch company was buying up all that Peter's factory could produce for its stores across the Netherlands. In a time of continued recession, when other furniture manufacturers were finding it difficult to secure work, Peter's company had a full order book. Soon all their outstanding debts had been paid and rather than making staff redundant they were able to employ a few more!

In one of his appreciative phone calls after that Peter told his spiritual mentor, "You always said that God would honour us for handing our business over to Him for His glory. We have tried, even through the darkest days to forward what we could to help with evangelical outreach. Now we are convinced that we are working for the best boss ever!"

Peter and Donna had been believers with a genuine desire to serve the Lord with all of their lives but August encountered someone with a completely different set of needs one evening when speaking at a Full Gospel Businessmen's International rally in Banbury, Oxfordshire.

He had been, as was his usual approach, sharing a personal testimony of how he came to faith in Christ and his subsequent experiences in Sign Of The Fish. These included instances of how God had called others to Himself for salvation.

When the meeting was over a number of people remained behind to ask August further questions or to assure him of their prayer support. As he was dealing with those nearest to him he became aware of a gentleman in his late sixties, possibly early seventies, dressed in a dark suit amongst those still waiting. This particular man attracted August's attention because he was shifting nervously from one foot to another, and he appeared to be alone. At least he wasn't speaking to anyone. He seemed so shy and unsure of himself. It was as though he felt he didn't fit, but was still determined to be there, whatever the emotional implications.

As soon as he could free himself from all the others crowding around him without causing offence, August went across to him. "Is there anything I can do for you?" he asked the jumpy gentleman gently, trying to appear as positive and reassuring as possible.

"It's just that I want what you have," was the instant and earnest reply.

"O.K. and what's your name so that we can talk?" August went on, wanting to set the man at ease.

"I'm John." Another curt response didn't help the would-be counsellor much further forward, but he would keep at it.

"Well, I'm August," he volunteered with a smile. He always found it easier to gain people's confidence when addressing them on Christian name terms. It was a trick he had picked up from living and working with Jill for so long. "What do you mean, John, you want what I have?"

"I want Jesus in my life in the same way as you have Him in your life. I know for a fact that I don't have the relationship with Him that you have," John confessed.

This presented August with a tremendous opportunity to tell this seeking stranger of the love of God and the death of Christ on the cross for our sins. When he had finished an outline of the Gospel message August told John that he could have Jesus in his life by believing in Him. This involved confessing his sin and inviting the Saviour into his heart.

"I want to do that now," was the anxious gentleman's reaction to August's explanation of salvation.

"That's great," August told him. "Perhaps the best thing I can do for you is lead you in a special prayer I have here on the back of this little booklet. You don't have to say these exact words to come to Jesus, but I find they help people express the feelings of their heart." With that he slipped A Fisherman's Tale out of his pocket and said simply, "Perhaps you would like to pray these words from your heart, John."

A nod of the head gave assent to the desire of John's heart. His eyes had begun to fill up with tears. Aware of this, but choosing to ignore it, August began, slowly, "Lord Jesus, I admit that I'm a sinner." Then he paused and John repeated it after him.

"Please forgive me. I believe You died on the cross to atone for my sins," August continued. There he paused again and John echoed huskily, "Please forgive me. I believe You died on the cross to atone for my sins."

August went on again, "Please come into my life and make me a new creature. Give me the power to live as a child of God."

There followed yet another pause, and another heartfelt repetition of these words.

"I believe You are the Son of God and I now accept you as Lord of my life. Amen," the spiritual counsellor concluded his pattern prayer and John concluded it after him in a voice breaking with emotion.

"I believe… You are the Son of God…and I now accept You as Lord of my life…Amen."

When both men raised their heads and opened their eyes, August could see from John's countenance that something momentous had taken place in his soul. There could be no doubt but that God had heard and answered that earnest petition. John had indeed become a new creation. It showed in the shine on his face!

Now that they both shared the same status as children of God and brothers in Christ August felt free to ask a few more questions about the man he had just led to faith. "Tell me a bit more about yourself, John," he urged. "Do you live around here? Are you retired, or do you still work."

"Yes I live in Bicester, which isn't far away," John now seemed more relaxed and happy to chat. "And I am retired. I am Father John Gibb and I have spent most of my life travelling the world in the diplomatic service of the Pope. I thought I was happy until I came to this meeting, August, and heard what you had to say. Now that I have met you, and have had a personal experience of Jesus Christ that I had never believed possible, I am happier than I could ever imagine.

Happier than he could ever imagine.

That was exactly how August felt, too. He felt like jumping up and running around the room shouting "Hallelujah! Praise the Lord!"

He resisted the temptation though, choosing to settle for the less demonstrative option of inviting John to 'come across to Lincoln some time and see us all at Sign Of The Fish.'

John took him up on his invitation about six months later and after August had finished frying one day they sat chatting at a table by the window in the upstairs dining room.

Although John didn't really realise it, that moment meant a lot to August. Or to use John's words of six months before, more than he could ever have imagined.

"God has prospered you in your business here, August," John remarked, having had his lunch in the restaurant in the middle of the day, and seen how busy it was.

August paused for a moment, and picked out one of the few copies of A Fisherman's Tale left in the rack on the table before replying. "You are right in one half of what you have just said and wrong in the other, John," he informed the man who had by then become a close friend.

"What do you mean?" John was forced to ask, rather puzzled.

"You are right. God has prospered the business. But you are wrong when you say it is *my* business. It's not my business. It's *His* business. Jill and I set out to run this little shop for God. Any success it may have seen, either in sales or in salvation, is due to Him, and not to us..."He could barely finish what he wanted to say, for he felt the tears coming, and he didn't want to be seen crying in public. In his own shop, in his fish-fryer's outfit, what would the people think?

When he had regained sufficient composure August pointed across to John with the booklet he was holding firmly by the corner, and remarked, "And you, my friend, are the proof of that!"

"Yes I must agree with you there, August. I am the proof of that. God changed my life the night I went to hear you tell the story of Sign Of The Fish," John admitted at once. He wasn't as self-conscious as the shop-owner, though, for he allowed a tear to roll freely down his cheek.

Stretching out a leg from below the table he struggled into his trouser pocket to pull out a handkerchief to dab it away.

Then he sniffled softly, "And I must be one of dozens."

The enthusiastic new convert was right.

He was.

OTHER BOOKS BY THE SAME AUTHOR

MY FATHER'S HAND

THIS IS FOR REAL

JUST THE WAY I AM

SOME PARTY IN HEAVEN

FIRST CITIZEN SMYTH

SOMETHING WORTH LIVING FOR

HOW SWEET THE SOUND

AS OUR HEADS ARE BOWED

ONLY THE BEST WILL DO

A BRUISED REED

BACK FROM THE BRINK

OUT OF THE MAZE

THE TANGLED LAMB

SOLDIER, SAILOR, LIVE OR DIE

I BELIEVE GOD

PAINTING THE TOWN RED

WHO CARES?